THE POWELL DIARIES

by

Bill Rogers

CATON

A CIP record for this book is available
from the British Library.

Published by Caton Books

Paperback ISBN: 978-1-909856-29-5

Cover Design: Bill Rogers
Design and Layout: Commercial Campaigns
Background Cover Image: canva.com
Editor: Monica Byles

First published November 2021
Copyright © Bill Rogers
First Edition

'The world is indeed full of peril, and in it there are many dark places; but still there is much that is fair, and though in all lands love is now mingled with grief, it grows perhaps the greater.'

JRR Tolkien, *The Fellowship of the Ring*

'You never know how strong you are, until being strong is your only choice.'

Bob Marley

Introduction

The extraordinary diaries on which this book is based were part of the estate of Marie Hussey, Kate Powell's niece and sister of the late Richard T Hurst, chairman of the famous Threlfall engineering firm in Bolton (see Kate's reference to this firm on page 276). They were bequeathed to two of Kate Powell's great-nieces, Margaret Jack and her sister Julia Guttridge. It was Margaret's husband, Alex, who brought copies to me in the hope that I might be able to do something with them. Shortly afterwards, Alex was diagnosed with motor neurone disease. Sadly, within two years he was dead.

At the time, I was already under contract to write the National Crime Agency series of police procedural novels. Once freed from that constraint, I resolved to keep my promise and to share Will and Kate's story with the world. Given the manner in which these accounts came to me, all royalties from this book will be donated to the Motor Neurone Association in memory of Alex.

Part 1
Will Powell

William Powell was born in 1867 in the hamlet of Prees Heath, Wem, in Shropshire. One of seven children, his father William was a bricklayer and builder on the Squire York's estate. The family were Methodist, and Will took 'the pledge' to abstain from alcohol. Will must have shown early promise as he was coached by Archdeacon Allen, who wanted him to go to Oxford. Unfortunately, the family lacked the resources to enable that to happen.

Will contracted rheumatic fever in his teens, the effects of which – including weakness and chronic dyspepsia – remained with him throughout his life.

By the age of twenty he realised there was no future for him commensurate to his education and ambitions, and so he left for Liverpool, where he took lodgings and found employment that would enable him to save enough money to emigrate to New Zealand, where one of his mother's brothers, James Gough, owned a substantial farm and additional land. This decision was spurred on by the advice of his doctor that the climate in the Antipodes would be much more conducive to his health.

On 1st September 1893, Will, aged twenty-six, boarded the Lutterworth, a three-masted sailing barque, bound for Wellington, New Zealand.

Diary of my voyage to New Zealand
1st September to 19th December 1893

Written for my parents & brothers & sisters, in the hope that it may both interest and instruct them in the life of those who go down to the sea in 'ships' and do business in great waters.

Friday 1st September

The hour of our departure so long dreaded has come at last. Who can understand the lethargy and misery that creeps over the man who feels that for a time, perhaps for ever, he is becoming an exile from his native land! May God grant that so great a sacrifice be not made for nothing. But for my health I would not make it.

I am glad that my parents, brothers and sisters are away this day. Their presence would be too painful. Yet when the cables creak, and the steamer takes us in tow, my heart is with them and with a dear friend on the quay who has been so good to me. I watch her through my tears until I can see her no longer, yet I stay on deck as long as I can see a little of my native land, thus spinning out the thread now so slender which binds me to it. Then I go below to make my berth comfortable and put out all the necessaries in case I am sick. It is a rough dirty evening but gradually becomes finer. My hardest day is over, thank God. I hope those at home do not worry about me.

The barque "Lutterworth"

Saturday 2nd September

The tug left us at Holyhead at 4am this morning. The rush of the waters and the noise of trampling feet on deck prevent sleep, but I shall become accustomed to it in time. I rise early to find the good ship with her canvas spread out like an enormous fan. A gallant show! I think we are all homesick on board. Jack Harrison[1] is very much so, poor fellow! It is his first parting from home. We had a good breeze in the morning, but it gradually fell, and in the evening we were becalmed. Everybody is very kind and the food all I could ask for. Not sick as yet. The day seems to stretch out for all eternity.

---

[1] Jack Harrison is the only other passenger. Suffering from consumption, now known as tuberculosis, he is also travelling to New Zealand for his health.

Sunday 3rd September

Becalmed! It seems no Sabbath to me. How I would like to be at Moreton Wood or Liverpool today! I know they are thinking of me at home. I shall never meet such friends in a foreign land. The *Lucania*[2] passed us early today on her first trip to America. This is a long weary day. Harrison seems very unhappy, and so am I, but it won't do to give in to it. I retire early and sleep very well for a few hours.

---

[2] RMS Lucania was a luxurious British ocean liner owned by the Cunard Steamship Line and was launched in February 1893.

Monday 4th September

A strong breeze sprang up in the night and we had soon a high sea. It was a queer feeling in the night to twist and writhe in one's berth as the vessel rolled, and then as she pitched head up and feet down, and vice versa, but I shall get used to it. After eating my breakfast, I became very sick. The least said about such a day, the better. Where I wished myself, I can't say. Harrison and I lay on deck all day and they might have pitched us overboard for all we cared. How we were laughed at to be sure. It was just 'nice nuts for the sailors'[3]. Steward very good to us. Turned in early.

Tuesday 5th September

All right this morning, with prodigious appetite. Breeze has fallen leaving a heavy sea and the vessel rolls fearfully. Seems terribly miserable and uncomfortable to the landsman. You would laugh to see us grabbing at our cups and plates at table and losing half our food. Apprentices still very sick and so is Harrison a little, but he and I are fortunate, and both recover thoroughly in a few hours. It was beautiful in the evening to watch the myriads of phosphorescent flashes of light in the water and along the ship's side. Even the porpoises darting through the water make a streak of brilliant light. I like Captain Carpenter, the 2nd mate and steward very well. I should not be surprised if I and the 1st mate fell out, but I hope not. We are antagonistic somehow! I hope that Harrison keeps up and gets on, and that God will bless us with renewed health and strength. If I could send my love to all at home and to Edwin[4] in Ireland, I would!

---

[3] Colloquial use at the time includes 'eccentric or hilarious behaviour' and 'sustenance'.

[4] Will's brother

Joseph Foster – 1st mate on the Lutterworth

Wednesday 6th September

Fairly into the dreaded Bay of Biscay, which does little to earn its reputation. Towards afternoon it blew very hard, bringing the long seas washing over us. What an insignificant thing is a vessel on the great ocean! Ours seems but a toy. It was laughable when Harrison and I looked at each other and said involuntarily, 'I wish I were at home'. After we recover our sea legs and can walk, we shall be better. One of the seamen has a bad cold in the eye[5]. I gave him some camomile flowers and poppy heads Mrs Colegate[6] had given me to make something to bathe his eye. There is no pity on board a ship and I feel very sorry for him as his eye seems so much inflamed. Evening spent talking to Capt. Carpenter who reminds me of John Morris! Poor old John! I hope I may see him again!

---

[5] Viral conjunctivitis

[6] Mrs Colegate was Will's landlady in Liverpool.

Thursday 7th September

Still a good breeze, but too much ahead, giving the vessel a quick lurching motion. She springs and jumps like something alive. Landsmen – stay at home unless stern necessity compel you to leave it. Day spent reading and 'holding on'. The captain is very good to us indeed, and I have nothing to grumble about in any way, excepting that I cannot sleep very well as yet.

Friday 8th September

Rise early. Had toothache in the night. Hope Polly has got rid of hers. Fine breeze. Now off the Portuguese coast. It is pleasant to know so much of the route as I do and have to thank my father and mother for the knowledge. Just a week from home! The passing hours have been so long, as yet it seems but yesterday since I left Liverpool. It is ever thus! The past is nothing, the future seems all! Feel more contented and settled. Getting my sea legs now! Air very warm, singlet and pants have come off already. Lat 42° 32′ N Long 12° 23′ W. We have lost time, you see, and are an hour behind.

Saturday 9th September

No day seems familiar, and so today does not appear Saturday. I clip the fowls' wings, which by the way come from Shropshire and are therefore very interesting, and they are turned out on deck. Twenty or thirty have been in a narrow coop and they consequently look miserable. The ducks (Shropshire ducks!) are worse still. Poor things. There is no comfort onboard for anyone, I think. Weather fine, smart breeze. Making a quick passage so far. It took 14 days to reach here last passage. Lucky passengers do it! May sight Madeira tomorrow! No ships in sight. Retire early and sleep well. Still sailors coming aft to brace sails always wake me. And so does the rattle of the rudder when becalmed.

Sunday 10th September

Sunday again! How are we to bear 13 more? Nothing to do but eat and sleep. Miserable Sunday! The air is very balmy and soft now. No twilight, darkness coming on quickly. We are about 2,000 miles from the Equator and it is hot now. How will it be when we overtake the sun! The voyage so far has been a splendid one and the captain is very pleased. All your prayers and those of Mrs Colegate are being answered, you see. After dusk, Harrison and I sat on the poop humming over some of our favourite hymns to make it a little more like Sunday. As I watched, the phosphorescent light sparkling at our bows and along the sides of the ship rushed through the water reaching a climax of its beauty in myriads of sparkling lights in our wake. I gazed on the deep dark blue of the sky, and the illimitable ocean stretching all around, and such a sense of the infinity of God came over me as I have seldom felt, and the old Hundredth came to my lips, and I sang it with all my heart. Then came 'When peace like a river', 'Jesus, lover of my soul', 'Let some blessings fall on me', 'For those in peril on the sea', and 'The old Hundredth' again. Just for the moment I forgot the ship, myself, and my companions, and was lifted out of myself to be brought back again by the sound of the bells (8 bells). Here I might close, but I should like to say that the captain and 2nd mate had gradually drawn up and joined in, and in the shadows of the main deck I saw some sailors creeping towards the poop. I dare say that it seemed like Sunday to some of those poor fellows. I hope that we may have more, but it is rare that humour is over me.

Monday 11th September

I rose today very stiff and sore. I fell down the companion[7] yesterday on the slippery brass steps but hurt myself very little. I am still lame today. I must take care when the vessel lurches. Vessel becalmed and rolling heavily. I had a good laugh in the afternoon. Passing the mate's door across which only a curtain was drawn, I was flung suddenly through it, and plunged with my head on to him in his berth! Soon afterwards the 2nd mate foolishly put his port open and was deluged with a heavy sea as he lay in his berth and both his and 3rd mate's bed were saturated. They had to sleep on the hatches all night afterwards.

Tuesday12th September

Rose late after a bad night! When becalmed, the rudder makes a noise like thunder. The recurring Boom! Bang! Crash! plays havoc with my poor nerves and consequently I hate the calm; I prefer a strong gale, I think. We sighted two sails to windward, and then we had a race, for a fresh breeze sprang up, before which we scudded along merrily. They crowded all canvas but speedily dropped astern, and by the night were almost lost to sight. The captain gave me a glass of beer tonight and I soon fell asleep. There is plenty on board, and I should have one sometimes to help me to sleep, but they charge 9 pence per bottle, and call it a favour. My conscience!!!

Wednesday 13th September

Tired and weary all day but going to abide by it as I have done hundreds of times before. I do hope I rest well or otherwise my sacrifices and that of my friends will be of no use.

---

[7] The companionway stairs lead from the deck of a ship down to a cabin or lower deck.

Thursday 14th September

Had a good night. None but an invalid can know how wonderful I feel for such a blessing! The sun beats down fiercely and for the first time we have an awning on deck. Too hot to move! The evenings are, however, beautiful. The sun goes down suddenly, and then from the Horizon upwards floods of glorious colours spread over the sky, and darkness is upon you. So different from old England where the twilight lingers and slowly ushers the day into night. The moon now shows itself shedding a silvery light on one broad line across the deep blue waters, and this broad line is a mass of broken light, as the moving waves transfer the light from crest to crest. These calm beautiful evenings will live in my memory forever.

Later I paced the decks for hours, thinking of the future. Anxious for my health[8] so that may do something to retrieve these wasted years. I am only wearing shirt and trousers now. No stockings or boots. They call me the living skeleton because I look all bones now my underclothing no longer rounds off a little. I tell them that I shall look fat when I land in New Zealand. These sailors are fine brawny muscular fellows. The 2nd and 3rd mates are like young Hercules and with great muscles, limbs and chests. I put on bathing drawers and regularly have a swill 'forrad' at the pump. I pump 3 or 4 buckets of seawater, and then get some of the men to throw them on me. A splendid tonic, helping me to sleep. We are well into the N.E. trade winds now and are making good way. We have a peg on board and a few rope quoits which we pitch over if we can, and with cards and draughts, and reading and an occasional yarn from the cook, the time begins to pass quite pleasantly.

---

[8] Will's weakness resulted from having had rheumatic fever as a child.

Bucket belonging to the Lutterworth

Friday 15th September

Take an hour's walk on deck before breakfast. Been dreaming of home all night. Edwin's holiday soon over and Aggie's[9] is over. The ship goes along well, plunging her head right under the seas, and then rising gracefully and shaking herself free. Neither pitching or rolling affect me now, and I can walk in any weather, my body writhing naturally with the motion of the vessel. I shall feel queer when I land, I know. I have turned out quite a sailor and should often go aloft and pull on a rope but for my promise to Mrs Colegate and all of you. It may be dangerous, but one is thought a chicken to fear going aloft, and I should like it. I wish I had not promised now. I did not promise any of you, but Mrs C extracted a definite promise as to what I should not do.

Have no appetite: too hot! Flying fish pursued by beneto[10] and dolphins are around us now. I wish they would fly on board. They are said to be good eating. I try

---

[9] One of Will's two sisters

[10] Almost certainly bonitos, also known as skipjack tuna, which are medium-sized predatory fish in the same family as mackerel and tuna.

to turn in at 12pm but have to retire to bed where I am bathed in perspiration, although I be in my berth stark naked. The heat of the decks and the iron at the sides makes one's berth precisely like Mother's oven when she puts in her hands before baking bread. The pitch boils up between the boards on deck. I stand it pretty well, being thin. It plays havoc with the fat ones.

Saturday 16th September

I dislike Saturday. I wish it would rain so that we could wash, or I shall dirty everything. Talk about only loving a change! One wants a change every day. Shaving day today! And it takes doing on board ship! This afternoon I cut Harrison's and the carpenter's hair. You would laugh if you had seen us. They swayed and I swayed. I made a cut and got too deep, and they bobbed out of the way. But I managed it by cutting off close all over to the head. My feet smart terribly. All the skin is burned off by the sun. Have made 220 miles today before a fine breeze. We have plenty of food and variety of diet. Breakfast: bacon & eggs, Irish stew, fish, curry with good cocoa come alternately. Dinner: fowls, duck, roast tinned beef, ditto mutton, corned beef, minced collops[11], tinned chicken, rabbit, oxtail soup, mulligatawny ditto, pea ditto. Potatoes, turnips, carrots. Apple pie, sago pudding[12], cornflour mould[13] and fruit come in their turn. Tea: – cocoa, brown bread, haddies[14], kipper, lobster, salmon, jam, marmalade, etc. So we have plenty

---

[11] According to Mrs Beeton's recipes, a dish of minced beef, lamb or venison, braised with onion and tangy seasoning.

[12] A sweet liquid milky pudding, thickened with the pith of certain tropical palm trees and flavoured with vanilla and cinnamon.

[13] Often almond-flavoured, blancmange is a sweet wobbly milk-based dessert, thickened with cornflour and set in a mould. This was a favourite when I was growing up in the post-war years. Try Mary Berry's recipe!

[14] Haddock, presumably smoked.

of choice, although I live plainly, and so does Harrison. I am so glad to say that he gets on wonderfully. The hot weather suits his chest. I hope he may still progress when we get into the bitter cold, 'Running the Eastings down'.

Sunday 17th September

A fine N.E. wind carries us 280 miles. Twelve similar days and we should reach the Cape, out of intense heat. This is a day when we miss our homes and friends most. The less said about it the better. The monotony seems worse on the Sunday when nobody stirs much but the sailors who wash and dry their clothes – poor fellows – as best they can.

Monday 18th September

A fine breeze again! Heat intolerable during the night below. Bearable on deck. I was standing on the forecastle head today watching the hundreds of fine fish, which dart from below the bows, but they won't bite. I am bilious today. Rather unusual for me.

Tuesday 19th September

Still bilious and the captain says I have erysipelas[15] in my left leg, which is swelled below the skin and covered with bright red spots which burn and pain very much. I think it 'prickly' heat, cold and exposure which results from having no clothing on my feet and paddling about the wet decks. I draw a veil over this day.

Wednesday 20th September

A veil over this day too! Becalmed! Heat fearful, and foot bad.

---

[15] A bacterial infection characterised by large raised red patches on the skin. Often mistaken for cellulitis or prickly heat.

Thursday 21st September

Foot better. Biliousness gone. On deck all day under an awning. In a steamer going at 15 to 16 knots, the rate of travelling makes some current. But when a sailor is becalmed in the tropics about 10 degrees N, then to quote the steward – 'By the Lord Harry, it's hot as Hell!' Nobody in England who has never left home can form any idea and I can't give one. Fortunately, it commenced to rain about 10pm as it can only rain in the tropics. Each drop, a bucketful! It cooled her sides and her deck and for one night I slept well and so did we all. None of us can sleep in this weather.

Friday 22nd September

Moving a little this morning! What a blessing is a breath of fresh air! Foot much better, thank God, but still much swelled. Porpoises are sporting round us in scores, rolling and tumbling and blowing, but not near enough to spear. A great shark came close astern but would not bite a piece of pork hung on a hook from the stern. Perhaps the great big fellow had tasted pork before. He looked with his wicked little eye as if he had got 'a nasty mind'. Harrison still keeps improving, I am pleased to say. The more I know him, the better I like him. He is quite 'Jannock'.[16] Quite a day of wonders today!

The first sound I heard on deck this morning was 'Sail on the Lee Bow!' How we ran to see it – just a speck on the horizon! Quite a wondrous episode in our history, relieving the monotony. We gradually overhauled it during the day, as we seem to overhaul everything before us. If the breeze is only just heavy enough to let her carry her canvas without shortening sail, this little ship can sail – but can't stand a press like more powerful ships. About 11pm as I sat on deck, a great steamer hove in sight. First came her mast light, then her green side

---

[16] Northern dialect for pleasant, outspoken, honest, genuine, straightforward and generous.

light, and then her row of lighted ports. She passed us homeward-bound from the River Plate about one to one and-a-half miles away. It was too dark to speak to her. Otherwise in 10 days or so, the Liverpool papers would have announced that the *Lutterworth* had been spotted by her at Lat 19° degrees N. What thoughts that vessel gave to rise in my mind!

About 2.30am I heard a hoarse call on deck and ran up the companion in my shirt to find us about 100 yards from the vessel we had been overhauling. She was *Emma* from Liverpool to Rio de Janeiro. We wished the captain a good voyage and when I rose this morning, she was out of sight astern. Harrison who sleeps more soundly than I was in his berth and I did not wake him.

Saturday 23rd September

Rose early. Washed changed and shaved. Light breakfast. Soup dinner. Cornflour tea. Writing, sleeping, reading and talking filled the day. Oh! And I washed my shirt & drawers having got a little water from the steward. I did it privately in my berth, having soaked them a few hours with Sunlight soap. I have cheek enough to think I can manage it best myself. Cold water, of course! Making very little way indeed today. If a good breeze would only carry us out of this terrible heat. It's bad enough for me, but worse for the others.

Sunday 24th September

A breeze from S.W. carries us 2 points from our course. That is about 22 miles. Move but slowly. Day very warm and oppressive but tempered with a slight breeze. Very little energy and very little appetite. A steamer crossed our bows to windward about 11pm tonight.

Monday 25th September

Will someone kindly send us a good breeze? I am tired of creeping along so slowly. Sail on the port beam, barque like ourselves. My greatest hardship this hot weather is the limited supply of water. Three quarts per day per man. In this I wash myself, find enough for the cook to cook rice, oatmeal etc. and all other foods, and then have the rest to drink, which anyone can guess is very little. The tanks are leaking, and we are all put on small allowance. This is to say at the least unfortunate, but what can't be cured must be endured. This has been a typical tropical day. If such skies were seen in England, they would think the end was coming. Dense black clouds roll around the horizon resolving themselves in places into a kind of lurid mass where lightning plays beautifully. Then one of them detaches itself and coming over to us pours its contents on us like a deluge. The sailors get wet through, but the fierce sun soon dries their clothes. In the evening they are merrily washing their dirty clothes 'forrard' and I go to listen to their droll speeches and yarns. Goodnight to you all in spirit.

Tuesday 26th September

Wind still unfavourable, coming almost ahead, and we have to tack and run to the eastwards. Consequently, we have to run 5 miles to make one. I wish we could get over the Equator where we could depend on regular winds. We may beat about in the heat for a fortnight. It is dark every night at 6 o'clock and the evening seems very long. I begin to feel stronger and to sleep better despite the terrific heat. I often think a great deal about you all and about your anxiety for me, but it does not do to give way to it, and keep my spirits up wonderfully.

Wednesday 27th September

Slept very well. Neither the noise of the rudder, the waves, nor the watch on deck affect me now and I can sleep through it all. The sky is overclouded and there is a strong headwind blowing which makes it delightful after the intense heat and glare of the sun. About 12 noon all hands turned out at the cry of 'About Ship!' The captain took the wheel and for an hour I worked like a Trojan, heaving here, hauling there, at the capstan and braces, while the men sang out as sailors do, 'Heave oh!', 'Away Boys!', etc. etc. I quite enjoyed the bustle and rush and the hours very quickly fled. I have taken advantage of the coolness to take more exercise today. Of course, we are on the other tack now, and running westward, wasting time. If the wind would only become fair, we should soon be where I want. Vivid lightning comes every day – such lightning as I never saw in England! I leaned over the side watching it for hours last night as it lighted the entire heavens on every side. I expect it would alarm poor old 'John' a good deal, but I do not think it is at all dangerous.

Thursday 28th September

Have slept very badly last night. We are fairly in the 'Doldrums' and have been for about 10 days. We made about 2,500 miles south and about 1,500 miles west in the first two weeks from home. I don't think we shall make 60°S this fortnight. It is very trying to the patience. Lightning, lurid skies, intense or oppressive heat, constant heavy rain is the order of the day, and we have still 500 miles to go to reach the Equator where we may expect the S.E. trade winds. We may go in two days or it may take a month. Don't we wish for a little steam!

I hope you are all well and not worrying about me. If I could only hear from you, I shouldn't mind. How thankful I shall be to get letters at the other end. May God bless and keep you all safely that we may meet again.

Friday 29th September

What applied yesterday applies today. Still drifting about. It is impossible to say whether I am improving as the intense heat prevents much rest and makes me very languid and weary. It is the last 6 or 7 weeks of the voyage as we run to the east that generally benefits patients.

Saturday 30th September

Rose early. Washed and shaved, and then changed my underwear and washed it. The steward charges 4 shillings per dozen for washing, and as long as I can get a little water, I see no fun in paying it. A homeward-bound vessel passed us this morning: the wind, which is sending her merrily home, is dead against us. A strong breeze it is becoming too! By turning-in time, we shall have a heavy sea running.

Sunday 1st October

One whole month gone! Just as I thought, we have had a rough night of it and have had very little sleep, for my body was too much twisted about for sleep. Being a headwind, the vessel pitched very much. The breeze continued through the day, often blowing very hard. It is welcome after the intense heat, though of course, it is against our progress. If those at home were on the vessel on such a day as today, I am afraid they would be very ill. She is tossing just like a cork in the great waves. I have often thought of you all today and wished I could eat my meals in comfort with you. Dishes and plates roll around on our table as if alive. I always look over my album every Sunday for an hour. It does me good. I am sure if Father only knew how precious his portrait would be to me, he would have had it taken. Goodnight to you all.

Monday 2nd October

Still running westward instead of southward. The breeze has moderated somewhat, and the vessel can be kept better up to the wind. The day turns out a most beautiful one and, as the heat is bearable, I spend about three hours walking the decks. Three weeks ago, with as much motion I could not stand on the deck, not to speak of walking on it, but I have my sea legs now. I have felt wonderfully well today for me.

Tuesday 3rd October

I turned in about 9pm last night. We usually rise about 6am, sometimes earlier, so we retire pretty early at night. The officers reported this morning that one of the Pacific boats from Buenos Aires had passed us about 11pm last night. I wish they had called me. I enjoy watching a big steamer pass at night. They look like a little town. I spent this morning in helping to move cargo forward. The vessel was too much on the stern, so we opened up the aft hold and transferred several tons (bag stuff) down the hatch for'ard. The work did me good. I get treated with every respect and so long as you do not sacrifice your dignity in manner and speech, you may do any little work about the ship with benefit to yourself physically and mentally. I believe I am beginning to recover fresh strength, thank God. I shall be better placed to say more definitely in a few weeks. I can give a good strong pull on a rope now, whereas when I first came on board to do so only invited bad palpitations. We are keeping more to our course as the wind has shifted, and I think we are catching a little of the S.E. trade winds. In a day or two we shall reach the 'line'. I hope Neptune will not interfere with us. Today has been a delightful day. The breeze soon kills the tremendous heat of the sun.

Wednesday 4th October

Late last night after writing in my diary we crossed the 'line'. Although I suspected that we were very near, it had been kept a secret from us all and it was with a start of surprise that I heard pistol shots to port and saw 'Neptune' come over the side in his wet garments, and long white dripping beard. He quickly came aft and after wishing the captain a very pleasant passage, demanded if there were any on board who had never before crossed the line as, if so, they must either pay a fine (a bottle of whisky) or be shaved. The captain said he believed there were and as no fines were forthcoming, Neptune immediately ordered his four policemen to search the ship and find the delinquents. Then commenced a scene of fun. Two of the apprentices and two of the forecastle hands had never crossed the line and one after another they were found, their faces daubed with soot & grease, spiced with pig manure, and then dipped head over heels into a large tub filled with dirty water. It was too dark to see much of it but there was plenty of laughing. They afterwards demanded that the passengers be treated similarly (a thing which often occurs), but I objected with so much dignity or something else that the chief officer commanded them to stand away from the poop and go for'ard. I told the men that neither I nor my companion could afford to give them whisky at 5 shillings per bottle. I know it was custom on all ships, and that I should be considered terribly mean, but as Harrison had said previously, little as I could afford it, he could not afford it at all, and it was as much for his sake as for my own that I refused. The worst feature of it was this, that the captain gets it out of bond at half the usual price and then charges 5 shillings for what you can buy ashore for about 2 shillings and 8 pence, so we should not have been giving it to the men but should have been putting 3 shillings and 6 pence on each bottle into the captain's pocket. I could see no fun in doing that when I was poor and getting nothing, and he is getting £350 per year.

Today has passed without any event but one to mark it. About noon a vessel (barque) passed us within a few yards, homeward-bound from Concepcion on the coast of Chile. We spoke to her. I waved my hand to those on board among whom was a woman – the captain's wife, I expect.

At the time I write (with tremendous difficulty) the breeze has almost grown into a gale and we are flying along with the seas one mass of foam. Oh, it is a grand sight, but terrible! I have felt very unwell all day today. It is always so with me. If I feel much better for a day or two, I am sure to drop very low again and it almost makes me lose heart. None but God knows how it worries and depresses to be ever thus. Oh, would He but help me to recover, how grateful I should be! Chronic dyspepsia[17] is truly a most wearing disease and seemingly impossible to cure.

Thursday 5th October

What a night we have had to be sure! Sleep was entirely out of the question as it was quite as much as I and Harrison could do to prevent ourselves being thrown headlong out of our berths, and we are both thoroughly tired out this day with writhing and struggling to keep in our berths while the vessel was rolling and pitching fearfully, and every few minutes shipping so heavy a sea that she trembled from stem to stern. I can liken this to nothing else but the crash of thunder. When a sea strikes her like that, it is as if ten cannons had simultaneously crashed into her.

The breeze has held out all day, every now and then increasing into a squall and then moderating. Tonight it has grown very strong again, and we expect another gale for several hours. I have no fear of it, but the discomfort is horrible and something that a landsman cannot possibly imagine. Our vessel is overloaded for one thing, and this with her smallness makes her labour terribly. To walk is impossible and to stand without holding on is equally impossible. I scribble this during a lull in the breeze.

We passed another vessel homebound this morning, the *Casablanca* from New Zealand. We signalled our name and destination. It is a comfort to feel that in a few weeks, if Edwin examines the shipping news, he will see that we have spoken south of the Equator.

---

[17] Chronic functional dyspepsia, now more commonly known as chronic indigestion, is a condition than can cause pain or discomfort in the abdomen, often accompanied by nausea, belching and bloating.

Friday 6th October

Although a stiff breeze has been howling all night with occasional squalls, it has not developed into a gale, and this morning the sun rose clear and bright, accompanied by a moderate pleasant wind from the S.E. A most beautiful day indeed, bringing with it much more comfort. We are getting the sun a little to the north of us now. I wonder, shall we get your side of it again?

Saturday 7th October

A bright and beautiful day with a fine breeze and everything to conduce to good temper, and even some enjoyment of the discomforts of sleep. Another fortnight and we shall - D.V. [18] - be out of the hot regions.

Sunday 8th October

Our 6th Sunday at sea. It looks like a long time to anticipate eight more before we can be free. When I feel better and more energetic, there is nothing so hard to me as to feel cooped up like a rat in a trap with only 26 feet to walk on, for the main deck is wet and sea-washed most days, and very slippery with bare feet. I feel today as if I would give worlds to have a walk up the shady road to Corra[19] and to listen to Mr Billing would be anything but a penance. All day long we have been gradually overhauling an outward-bounder, which was passed this evening after darkness had set in. She was so close that the 2nd mate hailed her, but we could make nothing of her replies on account of the wind and washing of the waves. I thought I made out 'Glasgow' and 'Valparaiso' but may have been mistaken.

---

[18] An abbreviation of Deo Volente – God Willing.

[19] Corra is an alternative name for the village of Calverhall, near Whitchurch, and close to Will's parents' home. He may be referring to Corra Chapel, which was rebuilt in 1879.

No vessel has passed us yet, while we have overhauled plenty. I am not surprised that the *Lutterworth* made the smartest passage to Wellington for five years. Of course, she cannot do it without the wind, but with similar winds we have overhauled vessels with 10 and 12 days' start.

This has been nothing like the Sabbath day. I dare say you have all thought of me as much as I have thought of you. I would have liked to have sat down to your dinner. We are getting dreadfully tired of tinned meats every day and our vegetables are finished. I shall turn in early to sleep while the weather is good. Goodnight and may God keep you all is my fervent hope.

Monday 9th to Thursday 12th October

I am obliged to group these days for nothing else has occurred to mark one from the other or to vary the monotony of existence. When at home and weak during the dark winters 4 or 5 years ago, I realised what monotony meant, but then it was added to by great mental depression. Thank God I am free of the worst form of that now and if I were not, I think the glorious sunshine would soon dispel it. With a light breeze and glorious sunshine, we have been gradually making our way south, but we have not yet left the tropics and today (Thursday) when I write this, the heat is terrific. I am getting so accustomed to it now after a month in the tropics that I can bear it well and I am sure that with a proper diet I could live in them. Yesterday all hands worked to take down the sails and put strong new ones in their stead, for in a fortnight we expect to be down in cold and snow and frost, in the same latitude as the 'Horn', only east, and where perhaps the heaviest gales and storms are felt in the whole world. We expect six weeks of such weather and with no fire down below and the skylight battened with wood (thus keeping out the light) and with the decks washed 2 or 3 feet deep in seas, it is not a very pleasant time to anticipate. Such singing and hoisting and heaving went on yesterday! I helped them as much as I could, but the heat was too much for anyone not strong. One thing I must mention, hearing a scuffle one night, I jumped out of my berth to ascertain its cause and had to undergo the torture of having a rat killed on my bare foot by the cat. It was dark as pitch and I shouted, I can assure you! The doors all around the cabin opened, but only to close again while the occupants laughed at me. It was not very pleasant, I can assure you. I carried the rat half dead onto the deck and threw it overboard, but I was too much on the qui vive to go to sleep when I returned to my berth. Rats, cockroaches and fleas are the abomination of ship life. I should think there are tens of thousands of them on the *Lutterworth*.

Friday 13th to Monday 16th October

The sun rose bright and clear this morning. The sea was calmer, and I took the opportunity to write my diary. It is impossible to keep that daily now, for we have got down into the latitudes where storms are frequent at this period of the year, and indeed from here to New Zealand, rain, cold, sleet and biting cold wind will be the order of the day. On Friday last, the wind veered to the south, this coming from the cold regions where ice and snow abound. We had previously had the wind blowing from the Equator or tropics and Thursday was a very hot day. Friday was fairly warm, but Saturday ushered in a very different kind of thing. The wind was due south. The cold biting blast fairly blew through me and my teeth chattered in bed. I hastened to put on boots, drawers, thick singlet, etc., but it was no use. So sudden a change after the tropical heat was dreadful. The sea rose and rose until the vessel was driving bows under, deluging the forecastle and all for'ard.

I cannot pretend to tell you how this kind of thing affects you when it does not make you sick – we were alright in regard to that – but then if you lie down you must hold fast to prevent being pitched out. If you stand up (well, you can't stand up). If you sit down, you can't keep the same place five minutes. You want both hands to draw your trousers on, and yet you want both to hold on with. You put your trousers on the floor and stand in them, then you make a dive with both hands to pull them up and find yourself in a heap, rubbing a lump as big as a marble on your head, which in some way has struck the door. Washing yourself is worse still. Eating is as bad. In fact, in bad weather you ought to be able to fall asleep strapped in your bunk and wake up when it's all over. Both Harrison and I would give all we have to be landed ashore, anywhere out of this discomfort. I do not wonder at Chas Gough[20] never returning to England. In a good-sized steam ship with electric lights, fresh meat and vegetables, and plenty of society, it may be managed for weeks, but 13 weeks in a small boat heavily laden like this, with nothing but tinned meats, no company, no fire, no light except to turn in with, pitching and rolling from day to day, is enough to make a man wish himself dead, and that's the truth.

Rain poured in torrents all day yesterday, and the sea was washing us fore and aft all day. Many a time I thought if Father and Mother could see me now, they would know how much I was going through for the sake of my health. This has been rather bad lately. Indigestion and weakness have been rather bad this last week, and I have hardly felt strong enough to crawl about. However, I am better today considerably, and if the weather will only keep good, I shall get some strength again. They all say if I had had a good turn of sea sickness, I should have been better and improved very quickly afterwards, but I have not been fortunate, and have been free from sea sickness in the worst weather. However, I may feel the tonic effects of the voyage after landing (D.V.).

---

[20] Probably Will's cousin, Charles Gough

Albatross, Cape pigeons, mollymawk[21] and hundreds of birds follow us from day to day, never resting. What tireless wings they must have! Oh God, how manifold are all thy works! Some of them are most beautiful. I shall try to catch and keep one or two of them if I can. They will follow us the 8,000 miles to New Zealand. We still have that far to go, having only come about 84 degrees from England, or about 5,000 miles, but then we shall get strong winds just now carrying us to New Zealand at a rapid rate. The worst of it is that we are going south, where there are often icebergs, in order to shorten the degree of longitude. We are 46 days out today and may expect to be 60 more. It looks like an eternity, but what can't be cured must be endured. I was prepared for anything when I set out, and I have got it, so I must not grumble. If fine, I shall write again tomorrow. My heart was with you all on Sunday – we had a most miserable day.

Tuesday 17th to Thursday 19th October

Three more days have passed. I have nothing to record unfortunately, for nothing has occurred. Certainly we have watched with interest the efforts a vessel, which has been in our company since Friday last, has made to leave us. We first sighted her on Friday, and on Saturday night we had her right to leeward on our beam. A head sea had been running all day and it was amusing to see her crowd all her canvas, dangerous as it was, in order to keep her lead, but it was of no avail. The *Lutterworth* is very clean-cut fore and aft and plunges into a head sea – bows under – in capital style. We lost sight of her until Monday when the sea fell, and she came up to windward, having stolen a march on us.

---

[21] Deep-diving seabirds related to the guillemot, puffin and penguin.

Monday and Tuesday, we raced all day without making any perceptible difference in our positions. On Wednesday morning, we were hugging the wind closer and we gradually edged up nearer, but of course, as she kept the wind a little more abeam, she began to gain on us and gradually drew ahead, a point and a half freer, so we lost her again to leeward. She was a smart vessel and no mistake, very much larger and finer than this, although barque-rigged.

The weather has been most miserable. On Tuesday, a heavy fog descended, and we were compelled to shorten sail and proceed more gingerly, being in the track of vessels. I never saw such a fog. I was only out for an hour or so, and my clothes were saturated. Towards evening it commenced to rain a most drizzling rain, and the wind increased, bringing a very strong sea up in a few minutes. I turned in about 9.30pm but not to sleep. There is nothing so trying as to be on a vessel almost lying to in a heavy sea. When moving, her sails keep her somewhat steady, but when she lies like a log, rolling and heaving and pitching, tossed back and to on the great waves, it is awful. For four mortal hours I lay in my bunk, expecting any moment to be pitched out.

As she pitched, I could feel myself going down, down, down, and then up, up, up, and perhaps in the middle of heaving, she would violently lurch. At last she gave a terrific plunge, and I heard the captain spring out and dash up the companion in his shirt. What he ordered I don't know, but she began to move a little and the rest of the night the motion was more bearable. I heard on the next day that she had plunged under the sea up to her foremast. For a moment I thought we were going to Davy Jones's Locker!

Friday 20th and Saturday 21st October

Wednesday and Thursday proved wretched days, and today is no better. Thick fog and drizzling rain from morn to night, with us cooped up like rats below, the skylight covered in, little light and absolutely nothing to do. I have felt I would give worlds to be ashore, but it's no use. Here we are and here we must remain for six to seven weeks, and it's no good to grumble. With health like mine, it is impossible to be other than very poorly under such conditions. The food lies on my stomach like poison or a lump of lead for want of exercise. However, I won't grumble in my diary. All that cheers me up is the thought of return: at home someday a better man...I hope!

Dense fog and rain, moping, melancholy, ennui unutterable, and these two days are set before you. The less said about such days the better. Miserable as they are now, I shall soon forget all about them when I put ashore.

Sunday 22nd October

When I awoke this morning, the sun was shining in through my port brilliantly, and in a few minutes, it had shed as bright a light into my heart as into my berth. I dressed and went on deck to find us no longer lying as a log on a heavy sea on account of the fog, but scudding along before a fine breeze at 11 knots per hour. How I have enjoyed the day! Talk about stretching my legs . . . I have walked the poop the entire day like an animal let loose after confinement. I soon got tired but that did not matter. I rested and had another spell, knowing that I may be denied the pleasure again for a week or two. Not one of you can understand the sense of pleasure or freedom that I have felt this day, because you have never known what confinement is in the same way.

Nearly all my thoughts have been of home and you all, and I have wondered at different times what you have been doing. My mind is much exercised as to the future, which may be as different as any conception I may have of it. Life in New Zealand is nothing like English life, and without influence from someone, I may be unable to get a living except at work altogether too much for me. But I do pray that God will lift the cloud which has hung over me so long and show me its 'silver lining'. With good health, I should be all right, but if I keep weakly, I shall only manage light employment. I do hope I shall find it. If not, I shall ask Mr Proctor to find it me among all his employees and return to England.

I am afraid that we have by no means done with the thick weather. The moon has a big misty halo around it tonight. We have just passed the island of Tristan da Cunha. I should like to have spent the day ashore.

Monday 23rd October

As I thought, it has proved a wet day. The mist is so thick as to fall like 'small rain', wetting everything through, and of course, we cannot proceed and be rolling on the trough of the sea. She goes down to the water edge, and sometimes lower, and back up again to dip the other side in. I should like to see any of you at home even stand on such a deck slippery with wet. Of course, you could get used to it as I have done. My body sways and straightens itself according to the motion but it's awfully uncomfortable. There is a very heavy swell here off the Cape, very different from what prevails just round the coasts at home. We are 1,000 miles off the Cape.

Tuesday 24th October

Quite warm, but wet and misty. Made very little progress indeed. I am thankful to say that I am feeling a great deal better than during the last few days. What a difference between the days in England and here. At home, they are gradually getting shorter. With us, they are getting longer but are at the same time bitterly cold when a south wind blows.

Wednesday 25th October

The breeze which sprang up at sundown last night, and carried us along during the night, fell this morning, and we are becalmed and may remain so until morning. The sun has shone brightly, and the sky has been clear and blue like the sea itself, which lies gently heaving, looking very little as if its surface could be lashed into great angry waves. Albatross and Cape pigeons hang very close to us, and today one of the boys caught a pigeon with a hook and long line and killed it for the sake of its beautiful wings. I would do so myself but cannot find it in my heart to kill such a pretty innocent bird. Many efforts have been made to catch the gigantic albatross, but to no purpose.

Wednesday evening, 9pm

The breeze has returned, and we are moving again. Although pretty warm today in the sun without a breeze, it is bitterly cold tonight, and it is in rain that I walk the decks rapidly to warm my feet before turning in. They were as cold last night as to prevent sleep and we have no fire, although the glass indicated this morning 4 degrees from freezing point. Goodnight – I wish my feet were at the old fire at home.

Thursday 26th October

This has been a very beautiful day, fairly warm and bright, with little or no breeze. Harrison and I after the exercise of much patience caught two pigeons, but lost one in getting it aboard. Instead of killing the other, we stamped our names together with the name of the ship and date on a small piece of linen, and then attached it to the pigeon's neck in the hope that someone else might fall in with it. The birds cannot alight, or if they do, they are caught fast, being unable to rise, and so they remain forever on the wing, only occasionally resting on the seas when very calm.

The sailmaker has been very poorly today, indeed ill, and although I would willingly do much for him, discipline does not allow it and I am obliged to content myself with making enquiries and bearing him company. He is a man I like as well as anyone on board. I had no sleep myself last night and so am feeling rather low. There is every sign of rough weather tonight, and I hear them taking in canvas, both mainsail and topgallants and royals. That means more discomfort for everybody.

Friday 27th October

I had a better night last night – thank God. When I rose this morning, the sounds of rushing winds and heaving waters struck my ears, and the difficulty of dressing quickly told me that rough weather has set in again. What a day we have had to be sure! Such heaving and rolling and tossing! Worse than ever! To give an example – Harrison was sitting on his settee at the end of his cabin with his back to the side of the cabin when a sudden lurch sent him flying off across the floor like a ball. Fortunately, he was not hurt. Every time we moved this occurred, and I believe that as a drunken man by means of his helplessness rarely hurts himself when falling, so we escape, for I have been flung about like a ball today.

At noon, tired and weary of sitting about below, we both went on deck and had only been on deck about ten minutes before an enormous sea swept us fore and aft and had we not both clung fast to the poop rail, we may easily have been washed overboard. Harrison was standing on the lee side of one of the small boats, and it will give you some idea of the height of the seas when I say that the sea went high over the boats and filled his clothes from his head downwards. I sprang on the rail, still clinging, and got hold of one of the lifeboats and was only up to my middle in the surging water. Of course, we both had to change everything. My boots were filled, and I had to wash them out with soap and water, or the seawater would spoil them. There is not a place to dry them, and they with our clothes must wait the first fine day and in the meantime be wet in our berths.

It is very cold. The snowbirds have made their appearance. The mate caught a mollymawk this morning: a great bird with a mass of black and white plumage, about seven feet from tip to tip of wings. He has killed it to make the feet into a purse.

We have no fire and shall have none whatsoever the weather as the fireplace is built up. It is very little use to speak of hardship and cold when all is hardship, so I forbear. We have only 6 more weeks to bear with it, and as it can't be cured it must be endured. As usual I made a great mistake coming out on a small old-fashioned comfortless ship like this! I live by making mistakes, although I do what I think for the best.

Saturday 28th October

I sat up most of last night. It was impossible to sleep for the roaring noise, and the seas struck us like thunder. To judge by the sound of pots and pans, there was some confusion in the steward's pantry. As to rolling, if you could go to sleep, you very likely find yourself lying with arms or legs broken as a result of rolling out of your berth. The seas are sweeping the decks, but I managed to get to the sailmaker for'ard. Poor fellow! None had seen him, and he was very ill. You may die and no hand stretched out to help. I gave him some medicine, which did him good, and I asked the captain to send him some beef tea as he had eaten nothing for two days. This with a piece of toast has made him better. Short a time as I was on deck, I had to clamber onto the top of the skylight to escape a heavy sea which swept over us. As it was, I was wet to the hips. I must take care I am not washed overboard, although I am wicked enough sometimes to feel as if I do not care what happens. It is very wrong to feel like that, but one cannot always help one's feelings. It will all be forgotten when we reach shore. I write this fastened on the rail of the seat of the cabin table.

Sunday 29th October

Another sleepless night gone. The seas have been washing right over us all night and although I did my best to wedge myself in my berth, it did little towards comfort. This morning I spent on deck, holding onto the rail and watching big seas coming 20 feet above my head and looking as if they would come right over us astern. Yet we just escaped, and they roll underneath instead. The spray, of course, flies all over us. We have had several squalls today with heavy rain. To hear the wind howl in a squall is enough to make anyone deaf. One struck us suddenly after tea (tea under difficulties). I was sitting at the end of the cabin, holding to the brass railing, when it came on us like a clap of thunder and I was hurled across the cabin like a rocket, striking my skull against the iron seat with force enough to make it black and blue in a few minutes. Fortunately, I struck my head into Harrison's body, who was holding to the other side. It did not hurt him and saved me from almost knocking my brains out. Gracie Beasley[22] have overloaded us, and in a heavy sea like this, it is torture to be on the vessel. Officers and all grumble fearfully. I suppose we shall get safely to New Zealand, but we have something to go through first.

Monday 30th October

Another night and day like the last two. I am almost wearied out for want of sleep. There is no true sea running and the motion is fearful. She almost threw me over the table at dinner, and the 1st mate had a lump on his head like an orange. He was flying across the deck and struck his head against a davit with great force. The captain's brother – master of the large ship *Nelson* – had his head fractured last passage out and died in Wellington, where he is buried.

---

[22] The loading brokers in Liverpool, Gracie, Beazley, & Co.

Bad as it is, and much as I dislike to be laughed at myself, I laughed until I am bad when I see anyone go like that. I am sorry to see them hurt, but their utter helplessness would make a pig laugh. They laugh at me whenever I am hurt or not. Indeed, no one could help it. It does indeed behove everyone to be very careful. She shipped a lot of sea today, which filled her main deck to the top of the bulwarks, submerging the galley and forecastle. I don't know how the pigs came off, but some men were almost washed overboard. Poor fellows – theirs is, I am sure, the hardest of all existences. Heaven help the good men who are working to ameliorate their 'condition'.[23]

Tuesday 31st October

The wind fell about 4am and, as the sea subsided, I went to sleep and had my first two hours for four nights. This has been a fine day, but I was too tired to enjoy it. Harrison sleeps in any weather and he ought to be very thankful for it. As we ran out of the current that prevails here, we got a truer sea and there is more comfort in consequence. The wind has veered considerably, and we are now heading SSW rather off course. I am turning in early tonight to try to obtain some much-needed rest. The last week or two has put me almost beyond sleep, as loss of rest weakens my nerves so much. I hope we shall have a spell of good weather so that I may not land in New Zealand very weak. It is bitterly cold. Harrison is recovering wonderfully, but his digestion is so much better than mine, which rebels against this food terribly. I am very glad he progresses and wish his mother could know. It would cheer her heart indeed. I hope against hope but am getting to feel very much disappointed. Never mind, God may send me better health soon.

---

[23] Will is probably referring to the Mersey Mission to Seamen, founded in 1856.

Wednesday 1st November

We have had a heavy storm for about nine hours. It roused me at 2am this morning and there was no more sleep to be had. The wind howled and the rain poured in torrents and we were soon reduced to bare poles. This lasted until noon today. Many a time the ship trembled with the force of the heavy seas last night and I thought each shock would break her up, but the captain only laughed and said it was nothing, though he was on deck almost all night and he never stays there and puts us under bare poles for nothing. To me it seemed awful and I thought of you all so comfortable and secure in your beds. An albatross was caught this morning: 14 feet, 3 inches, from tip to tip of wing. It took six men to pull it aboard. I went to look but had to go below, as it was very dangerous to be on deck. I have spent the afternoon and evening on deck, although of course, I could only stand still and hold on. Anything is better than to be confined below. There is another night of rolling in my berth before me and no sleep. I shall not turn in very early.

Thursday 2nd November

The weather changed during the night and I fell asleep about 4am. We rise about 7 for breakfast. The day has proved a very beautiful one and although very early, I have much enjoyed it. About noon, Harrison and I caught a beautiful albatross[24] 11 feet from tip to tip of wings. With help we got him on board and the carpenter skinned him. The breast is most beautiful and when cured makes a magnificent tippet or muff. The skin of the feet makes a very nice tobacco pouch and the upper bone of the wing a beautiful paper knife, while the lower bone makes a handsome pipe stem.

---

[24] Presumably, Will had not been put off by Samuel Taylor Coleridge's epic poem, The Rime of the Ancient Mariner [1798]!

These parts were soon claimed, as we knew not their value. But if we catch another, we shall keep it. I want to get a tobacco pouch from the feet, have it mounted and send it to Edwin as a curiosity. There has been very little breeze today. There is, however, a very heavy swell on after the storm and this causes a most trying motion. I hope we shall have a few good days that I may get more rest and sleep.

Friday 3rd November

Still rolling about on a swelling sea. With some difficulty I got a little exercise on deck today. It is what may be called walking under great difficulties. Still I suffer so much from indigestion without exercise that I am compelled to obtain some. This afternoon we caught a mollymawk and took off both feet and skinned them. I tore one and got the other off perfectly, but in opening the folds of skin with a spoon, I tore it. I was disappointed as they do make a pretty pouch. We must try again! This is the only relaxation we get. How we shall jump for joy when 'land ho!' is cried from the forecastle head.

Rain came down pretty sharply this afternoon and evening, but I was so tired of being below, I stopped on deck and got wet. It is 9 weeks since I left Liverpool and it looks like 9 years. The rats have carried a shirt away from Mr Law's room (the mate's) and I am obliged to keep a sharp look in my own berth. There are hundreds of them on the ship, and they poke their noses everywhere. I prefer their room to their company.

Saturday 4th November

The wind veered south this morning and was consequently bitterly cold. It has gradually grown in force until we are at 8pm making about 13 knots. The masts writhe and bend under the press of canvas, which the captain is carrying as long as possible to make up for the last few days' delay. I have had some words today about the provisions. They have all eaten at our provisions until they are consumed, and now want to deny us fresh tinned meat and bacon. One and a half lbs of the latter per week allowed each of us by Gracie Beasley, and about one and a half lbs of tinned meat per day. We had bacon three times per week the first fortnight and then had none at all through the tropics being too hot, so that we had not had six lbs of the 40 sent on board. The officers and captain have eaten at it and, now it is done, want to put us off with 'Oh, your bacon is finished' and ditto with the meat, wanting us to come on pickled stuff. However, although Harrison would say nothing, I spoke pretty strongly today, and I fancy no more 'bluffing' will be tried.

The more I see of the world, the more I see it is everybody for himself, and let others go to the wall. I know we shall consume not half our provisions and, of course, that saves the ship's provisions and makes it good for the captain and steward when they arrive home. I have lived very hard since I came aboard, as there is very little of food except bread that I dare eat. However, what I can eat, I mean to have as long as it belongs to me, and if others eat it, I shall demand a substitute. We had no bother for I quietly and firmly said what I had to say, and the captain was very nice afterwards, and said he meant nothing. If he didn't, I was wrong, but putting many little things together which Harrison and I have noticed, I fancy it was all meant if I had only submitted.

We have spent most of the day walking the deck, taking advantage of the fine weather overhead. I shave regularly but I would advise anyone but a teetotal to try it. The seamen let their beards grow. One of them has a terrible bad hand. I am afraid the poor fellow will lose it! 41 degrees South, 35 degrees East.

Sunday 5th to Wednesday 8th November

Saturday and Sunday nights proved nights of sleeplessness, but on Monday night I slept, and have done so as I am in 'despair'. Asked the captain to let me have half a dozen bottles of beer to try to obtain sleep by drinking a glass each night. He very kindly (sarcastic), let me have them out of his kindness! Charged me 1 shilling a bottle. Such is man's 'inhumanity to man' that capital must be made out of another's suffering. However, they procured me 3 or 4 hours at the commencement of each night, and were in consequence worth untold gold to me. To add to their efficacy, Sunday, Monday and Tuesday were three beautiful days cold and clear with no breeze or sea & we lay as though in port. Although I could see the captain chafed at the delay, I thanked God, for I cannot sleep when there is so much motion as we have had recently. There has been nothing, of course, to mark the days from any other. Three gigantic albatross were caught on Sunday evening, and immediately skinned. One was 17 ft 4 in from tip to tip of wings. When brought aboard, they have their wings immediately locked in each other and being helpless on their feet, they are consequently harmless. Otherwise, a blow from their wings or their terrific hooked beak would lay anyone out. It takes 5 to 6 men to haul one aboard.

I do not think I have said how they are caught. A piece of strong brass is cut, the angles inside are covered with fat pork tied over the brass. A large piece of cork to keep it afloat is tied to this and a strong line, and then hove overboard. The albatross dives into it and usually drives his beak into the angle. With a sudden haul, he is then fastened so, his beak wedging into the angle, and is drawn aboard if his beak or brass do not give way.

The man's hand is better but still bad. He shows it me each day. He gets no sleep day or night for the intense pain but, being a human being, he does not need anything different from the terrible coarse salt food to invite his appetite. Poor fellow! I would share with him if I dare.

Wednesday morning brought a breeze, which steadily increased. Unfortunately, it is a head wind and will drive us south amongst the ice. The motion is worse too than a running sea. In fact, they are the worst seas a vessel has to contend against and tonight (Wednesday), I hope it has reached its maximum and will die away, although I fear not. The cold has been intense today. The air has been down to 42 degrees and with a powerful south breeze you cannot conceive how cold this is at sea. Anyone who has been to the Isle of Man in summer can understand it. It drives straight into the marrow of the very bone. My feet and legs went so bitterly cold that I had to go to the sailmaker's room for'ard and put my feet against the cook's galley, which adjoins his room. Coming aft again in the darkness, I was thrown across the deck by a lurch and got a blackened shin, but was thankful to escape so lightly. 10pm – The wind has risen very much, and the glass has fallen very low. I anticipate a very severe storm.

Thursday 9th November

Unfortunately, I am not disappointed. I wish I could describe a storm at sea. If I could, I would. But words fail; I cannot find them half graphic enough in their descriptive power. It commenced to blow very hard about 12pm, and from that time, I had to wedge myself into my berth and hold fast. Everything in my drawers was turned topsy-turvy. A wooden partition about 9 inches high divides my berth from the side of the ship leaving a span of about 1 foot. In this space I stowed away my books, boots, etc. They were flung out, and right over me. This may seem impossible to a landsman, I know, because he cannot conceive how far a vessel must lurch to pour things out of a deep recess behind anyone. The noise was deafening. A very pandemonium! The seas struck the sides of the ship with the noise of artillery, and she trembled! How she trembled. Those terrific spasmodic trembles in every plate and joint are exceedingly pleasing, I can assure you. You are charmed with the sea. Yes, it is grand! When you are not on it, though!

At six o'clock, I got up and tried to collect my scattered things when – hey presto! – she gave a most fearful lurch. I don't know how I held on, but I did. I heard a stifled shout and looked out to find the 2nd mate had been pitched headlong into a lazarette – the rear part of the hold, where stores were kept – the hatch of which had been taken off. At the same time, everything in the fore cabin (where Edwin saw our flour) had been flung in a heap. Sails, barrels, potatoes, vinegar and boxes, etc., lay in a confused heap. In the 1st officer's room, the drawers of his chest had been flung right out across his room and into the passage as if they had been shot there and emptied of their contents. On deck, one of the men was washed from what he had grasped into the scuppers, and wedged under a spar, from which he was dislodged by ropes, severely bruised but with no bones broken. The sea swept over the main-trunk 30 feet up her masts and came down on deck like thunder.

We got up at 7.30 and tried to wash in about a pint of water, but water and bowl were flung out of the stand. We got a little porridge and turned in for the day as much the safest place. About 10 o'clock, a sea swept right over our poop skylight, forced open the companion, and came right into our room. If the companion had not been instantly closed, we should have been flooded out. As it was, it was soon wiped out. It seemed awful to be in the bunk holding on for very life, but what about the poor fellows on deck, which is full up to the top of the bulwarks! I don't know which is worse – to be cooped up below in darkness (for the skylight is covered) with nothing to do, or to be on deck.

About three this afternoon it subsided, and we commenced to roll very heavily, there being no wind to steady her. I write this at 11pm, and if I had been told that I would write at all under such circumstances a few months ago, I would not have believed it. I fasten my inkpot to the table with studs and myself to the seat and then snatch at the writing as she gains her equilibrium for another roll. I wouldn't do it at all, but it passes away an hour or two and I am keeping several diaries to fill up time for amusement. I wish you all goodnight in fancy, and through the medium of the diary. I would not wish the poor old dog to have a night such as is before Harrison and me, and yet we are becoming so used to it that we don't make ourselves unhappy about it. I forgot to say I had a heavy fall on deck about 4 o'clock. I went up for a minute and was immediately thrown to leeward and must have been thrown overboard as the poop rail is very low if I had not allowed myself to fall flat on my back. I quickly retired below with a blackened hip.

Friday 10th November

Another very bad day. I lay in my berth until dinner. Before the head sea had gone down from yesterday's gale, another rose from the opposite quarter and blew great guns. We have consequently a cross sea and are shipping water on every side. The cold is intense. Glass has fallen to a temperature of 32 degrees. I have two pairs of socks and drawers on, and cardigan, jacket and a big coat, while my legs are wrapped in a rug, and yet I am perished. All we can do is sit in a heap and bear it. The cabin is in darkness, everything having been boarded up. We asked for the cabin to be lit but couldn't have it. Such is life!

We have been driven far from our course by the terrific gale, and a sharp lookout has been kept for ice, which must be in the vicinity by the intense cold. I am almost afraid of telling you my experience on this vessel for fear you should think I have been miserable, but I can assure you that long suffering from weakness has made me very patient, and so except when sleeplessness and weakness have made life a very burden, my spirit has risen above the monotony, the disagreeable food, and many other discomforts, and even the intense cold, and I have kept fairly happy. 'God tempers the wind to the shorn lamb.'

Nothing hurts me so much as to see Harrison, who is terribly sensitive to the cold as all consumptive people are, suffer so much from the cold. He may get much more comfort when below if the cabin door were shut, but they won't allow it. Those who are well have little sympathy for such as he. The sailors will have it that there is a 'Jonah' aboard, and account in that way for the continuous calms and gales alternately without so much as a single good day's run before a good breeze, which have prevailed for three weeks where the best running may be expected. They are awfully superstitious. I should not like them to fancy that I have been unfortunate, they would ascribe all manner of natural phenomena to the fact they had an unlucky person aboard. At the same time, there are probably those on the ship who have had much misfortune beside myself. The best way is to let no one know anything about myself. There is much sickness aboard, five of the crew being laid up. Fortunately, three of them are boys.

Saturday 11th November
A heavy sea with little wind. Feeling much better.

Sunday November 12th to Friday 17th [pages missing]

Saturday November 18th
We crossed the 180-degree meridian three weeks ago. The distance is exactly halfway around the world and although three times that between England and the

Cape, it is usually done in less time as strong west winds prevail, driving the vessels before a running sea an average of 270 to 300 miles per day right down to New Zealand. We made a good passage to the Cape, but have been driven hither and thither by gales ever since and have not even had a wind with a little Westing in it. Last voyage she had a bad opening to the Cape and finished well, and this voyage it is vice versa, so we shall be out 100 days where we expected at the Cape to be 85. The average passage is 100 to 110 days. Thursday morning I spent in walking the poop deck for 4 hours. I felt much better than usual. Of course, I sit down for a few minutes to recover occasionally and then I only stroll. I found a warm place under a sail where the sun caught me in the afternoon, and I slept two hours. I awoke chilly but refreshed. I am so thankful of sleep for I have suffered terribly from insomnia since I left Liverpool. I am improving nicely again now.

Evening on Thursday and morning of Friday (indeed the whole day) were spent walking and resting in the glorious sunshine. I felt wonderfully bright and hoped it would continue right to New Zealand. A fine breeze came on Thursday night and all day on Friday and up to noon today, when it increased considerably and blew steadily, and we made our longest run of 270 miles. In 15 days we should land if that would last, but tonight I can hear the officer on watch singing out 'Clew the Royals!', 'Haul up your mainsail!', 'Haul down the mizzen staysail!', and I fear we shall have more wind before we have less. Since noon the spray and the sea have been flying right over us and I have been busy darning drawers and socks. This morning I cut the captain's hair and trimmed his beard, which he has allowed to grow. I also cut Harrison's. I am much in demand for this. I have had a shave, a wash and now am about to turn in, hoping to get a better night than last, which proved to be a very bad one. I have no medicine here, so it is a case of Nature fighting to get well. I hope she'll win when she has the bracing climate of New Zealand to help her. In spirit I wish you all, dear parents and brothers and sisters, 'Goodnight'. It is 3pm with you. We have gained five and a half hours on your time.

Sunday 19th November

We had a very severe gale last night, which lasted about 10 hours, and no sleep could be procured by anyone. The wind accompanied by hail and rain whistled with a noise like that of the whistle of the Clan Line steamers at Liverpool, and Edwin can explain what that means. About 4am, I thought she would carry her masts away, but we were once more carried safely through it. Of course, we were confined below all day in consequence, as the sea ran mountains high, and we have rolled something frightfully: once set ashore we shall soon forget all about it, I don't doubt. It will be just like a dream. It is useless to tell you what such a day is like, so I shall conclude my diary today with 'Goodnight to you all'. I don't doubt you think often of me, and are much worse troubled about it all than I am.

Monday 20th and Tuesday 21st November

Two very enjoyable days. The weather beautiful and a fair wind. How I enjoy such days. I begin to like to be at sea very much and shall almost regret to land. If the weather would only permit being on deck always, I should be quite happy. Such is human nature! The brightness of the weather, the bracing and invigorating and life-saving breeze, the sea with its beautiful white crested waves dancing hither and thither, and the feeling of almost buoyancy which is generated by such a combination of happy circumstances entirely dispel the memory of storms and gales and darkness and utter discomfort, and I almost feel sorry that such a fair wind must, if it last, soon carry us to New Zealand. We roll constantly all the time when the wind is aft, but by practice I am now able to walk the poop when any one of you would not be able to stand. I shall surely feel very queer when we get on 'terra firma', after the weeks of walking on a heaving, rolling vessel. I am feeling better now than since I left Liverpool, and sincerely hope I may continue to do so.

Wednesday 22nd to Sunday 26th November

Between this and the time we reach New Zealand I shall have little to tell you. We expect to be there in about a fortnight and as not a thing happens to vary the character of my diary, I expect you will be thoroughly tired and weary of reading it. The weather has been beautiful with fine breezes excepting on Friday & Friday night when we had a very severe gale. We have had a number of gales but fortunately not very long ones. They are terrific for a few hours and then die away in an hour. We have more progress in the last few days than in the three previous weeks and we now lie under the lee of land. I mean Australia, which is about 500 miles to the north. Of course, we give the land a wide berth on order to round Tasmania, and to prevent any danger of being driven ashore should a southerly gale drive us before it for several hours. I often think of these words in the 107th psalm when a heavy storm comes upon us. I can fully realise them now. Please read them and see how true they are. You will find them in the middle of the psalm commencing 'They that go down to the sea in ships'[25].

---

[25] 'They that go down to the sea in ships, that do business in great waters; These see the works of the Lord, and his wonders in the deep. For he commandeth, and raiseth the stormy wind, which lifteth up the waves thereof. They mount up to the heaven, they go down again to the depths: their soul is melted because of trouble. They reel to and fro, and stagger like a drunken man, and are at their wit's end. Then they cry unto the Lord in their trouble, and he bringeth them out of their distresses. He maketh the storm a calm, so that the waves thereof are still. Then are they glad because they be quiet; so he bringeth them unto their desired haven.' Psalm 107 KJV v23-30

What brave men must Tasman and Captain Cook have been when they came down here without charts and any guide whatsoever in search of new lands.

The men have been scouring the teak wood and holystoning[26] the decks, which look beautifully white now and are less slippery. The captain has been uniformly very kind and considerate lately, and by watching closely I find the steward was more to blame than the captain over the few words we had. The steward is constantly grumbling to him about the provisions, etc., because he is so terribly mean in disposition. At the same time there was twice as much as we wanted but it has been consumed among the lot of us. It is impossible to get strength on our diet, which consists entirely of oatmeal, bread, Irish butter that the tropics has not improved, corned beef and cocoa. The potatoes are done, and I dare not eat the preserved vegetables, hash salt meats, dry hashes, tinned fish, curry, stews, etc., which the officers with stomachs like iron can eat and relish. They murder me. But for this I should like to be several more weeks at sea. As it is, however, the sooner Harrison and I are ashore the better. He is not so well as in warm weather. I often pray he may recover but I doubt it. His lungs seem to be extensively diseased.

I have been sleeping better, thank God, but cannot get much strength until I get more suitable food. It is Sunday night now and the captain is teasing me with a prayer book which he wants me to conduct prayers from. He is only teasing me. It has been a beautiful day indeed. Most brilliant! It is only dinner time with you. I wish I were sharing it with you. Oh dear, I can't go on for the captain. Goodnight.

---

[26] Scrubbing teak decks with a pad of crumbling sandstone. 'Holystoning' may be so called because sailors had to kneel, as if in prayer.

Sunday 3rd December

Our hopes are doomed to disappointment for unless there is a great change, we shall spend another if not two Sundays on board. From Wednesday until Saturday in the past week we have been near Tasmania (the Garden of the South). We crossed the Great Australian Bight before a rattling good breeze and reached about 138 degrees East when the wind dropped light and became dead calm. Lying within 100 miles of land and brought north by fairer winds where the summer is near its height, the weather had been brilliantly fair with the glass going 'up' into the mizzen top, and the sea like glass for smoothness.

This has suited Harrison and he is improving again, but whether I can sleep better without that 'regular up and down motion', I doubt. It is so dreadfully monotonous, and the food has become so unsuitable now the vegetables, bacon and meat (except that pickled in brine) and oatmeal are finished that I shall be glad to get ashore. Bread and butter is my staple food now every meal, and the latter is much too 'strong' to agree with my stomach. If only I could have proper food and nourishing, I feel sure I should get on splendidly, for despite every drawback I am gaining a little flesh and my cheeks are looking wonderfully fuller. It is when I get ashore and can command food which will better agree with this wretched stomach of mine that I expect to derive benefit and to feel the tonic effects of the voyage in renewed strength. As it is, I am tempted for a change to eat a little salt meat or fish with preserved vegetables at dinner time and immediately swell up to such an extent afterwards that I cannot even button my waistcoat, while the pain is unbearable. Harrison, poor fellow is just the same, so we can sympathise with each other.

Everybody is getting sick of the long voyage and the 'grub' and I am not the only one longing to get ashore. Indeed, I am often told I am the most contented, but I don't say all I feel. The ship is being cleaned fore and aft ready for port and one has to be careful to avoid the paint. I have done a tremendous amount of reading, having read everything of my own and what Edwin so kindly sent (Mr Proctor too) and all I could lay my hands on of everybody else's. At night the captain and I generally play cards for about two or three hours and we have Harrison to join us. I don't know what the captain will do when we are gone. He spends all his time with us on deck or below, and many a bit of fun we have. I could tell of many a lark he and we have been up to, and of many a happy hour spent forward in the dogwatch with sailors who spin yarns (often big lies), sing to a fiddle and generally amuse themselves. It is not all unpleasantness at sea and for some things I shall feel sorry to leave the old ship.

A light breeze sprung up last night and we are making 4 to 5 knots perhaps. We are but a week's sail from Wellington if we had a wind, but I am afraid we shall be 10 or 11 more days. When I get there, I shall have much to say of the new country which will interest you as I will not weary you with this any longer. Fancy the thermometer at 90 degrees on Thursday and this is December!

I often feel sorry that I cannot ease your mind about myself and my safety. I know you worry yourselves, but I hope not too much. If I had not been so stupid, I should not have promised to spend £1 on a telegram when the office will know by wire as soon as we arrive, and Mrs Colegate by calling can learn more than my own word 'safe' will tell her. If I fail to keep it now, you will conclude something is wrong and it will be a source of worry to me to know that you are very anxious, but it would be better for me to keep a pound, which God knows I may want as everything is terribly expensive in New Zealand. I hope you will think of this and tell me not to mind in your letters, which I am waiting very eagerly for and which are at Wellington now. God bless you and keep you all is my earnest wish.

Monday 4th December

I knew yesterday that we were near Tasmania, but I was not prepared for the sight which met my eyes on going on deck this morning. I immediately looked all around as usual and there right off the post beam was land!! The coast of North Wales was dwarfed by the grandeur of the southern coast of Tasmania. Lofty mountains towered into the clouds, while numerous islets and gigantic rocks rose out of the sea within a few miles of us. Indeed, we could see the foam as the seas broke over them. As the sun rose higher and higher, it gradually threw its light down the dark side of the mountains, lighting up the sombre brown of the rocks and making more distinct the deep valleys and indents between the gigantic summits which loomed up to the east and west as far as the eye could see. I thought I never beheld anything so grand. Aggie will know what it is to look at the Caernarfon mountains and Snowdon from the Anglesey side. Well, it was much better than they, and grander, and I need say no more.

Such scenes always move me indescribably, but after 14 weeks on the wide ocean I cannot tell how I was moved, nor of the emotion that stirred me at the sight of land. It quite took my speech and almost my breath. Old seadogs are the same and there can be no surprise at me. The novelty of seeing New Zealand appear will be lessened now. I have been feeling wonderfully well for me and I am not nearly as thin and shall have to sell two of my small coats. I expect to get more for them than I gave, as clothes are very dear in New Zealand and when a ship comes in, there are usually customers for any clothing which there may be to sell. The day has been beautiful, but the breeze all too light. It is five days' sail from Wellington. I wonder how long we shall be.

Thursday 14th December

In Cook Strait between North and South Island, New Zealand. We sighted Cape Farwell yesterday and with a fair wind gradually rounded it and drew into the Straits, which range in width from 80 to 90 miles. The coast on each side is simply grand. Great cliffs and mountains rise right into the clouds and in the background can be seen peaks twice as high as Snowdon. I would not do it justice if I were to try to present its beauties so I must leave you to imagine it all. I write this in the morning when with our present fair wind we may expect to reach Wellington tonight. I say expect, as it is by no means certain on account of the treacherous nature of the wind and the character of coast, which is too gigantic to allow of a side wind, and consequently you have either no wind at all or it is dead ahead or dead aft. It draws through these straits as through a tunnel and it is not uncommon for ships to be beaten back here for a week at a time, and many a gallant vessel has been boxed up here and driven onto the sunken rocks and great rocky inlets which abound on each side of the narrower parts of the Straits. Of course, if a head wind be moderate, it is possible to tack and beat through the Straits gaining a few miles on each tack, but unfortunately the winds in New Zealand are generally no mere half winds but often gales. I do hope it will not change for a few more hours when we shall be safely in harbour. I do long to see my letters and to go back into the world again!

The weather has been tropical since we left Tasmania and the sea almost like glass. We have crept along at about 100 miles per day. I would rather move faster, but it is better for Harrison and more than compensates for the severe weather we encountered for three weeks from the Cape. Indeed, I believe such sunshine and calm weather is unprecedented, and must have come for Jack's sake. It is making the passage terribly long, however, and the food is quite sickening for all of us. I don't want to see tinned dry stuff for many a year again! The meat is like stewed string that Bovril or other meat extracts are made of it before it is tinned, and we have no vegetables at all. After leaving Tasmania I had a heavy drawback as I could not sleep for five days and eventually had to take opium, but I am pulling up a little now. It is terribly trying just when one feels that one is making headway, but it must be endured.

I have been very busy helping to clean the ship, and although the officers made fun of the idea that I could paint, I soon had all the most particular and best work to do. I have made the saloon look very nice and have painted the captain's room in two colours for a change – light pea green mouldings and white panels, and very nice it looks, worthy of all my trouble and care. It in no way takes from my position on board and passes away many weary hours, which would be otherwise be very tedious. The captain's kindness of late could not be surpassed and he has done his best to make the ship a home for us.

Thursday evening, same day

Oh, how disappointed I am! I thought I should be lying in my bunk tonight reading the letters from all the dear people in England, but it was not to be. The wind has veered and it is right in our teeth, drawing us back into the wide part of the Straits to run from side to side and wait for a fair wind, which may not come for days. It is very exasperating. Had it been moderate, we might have beaten through, but it commenced to blow against us at 12pm and rapidly became a small gale, and we are heaving and tossing in a heavy sea which lashes the decks fore and aft. We have to wear ship every four hours and run to the opposite side of the straits under main and fore topsails. Heartsick though I feel at the delay, I cannot help but laugh at the sailors grumbling and swearing. The latter is a good sign, however. They do say it's all safe when the sailors swear. I hope it will not get too heavy so that we cannot stand it on the beam and have to run out to sea. I don't like the look of the coast and the rocks and islets lying about all unlighted. It's a terrible dangerous coast here, but we have come through many a danger safely and shall meet this one and overcome it. I have no fear. You are my greatest source of trouble, as I know what Mother is. She will worry when I am safe as houses. If I could only let you know, I should feel fairly happy.

Saturday 16th December

The gale continues. The captain has not turned in for two nights and I have had no sleep in consequence of the bad weather, and none of the men on deck when working the ship. The seas broke in through the skylight yesterday morning and flooded the cabin two or three inches deep. I sprang out and was paddling about barefooted in my shirt, rescuing my boots, cap and sundries, which had been flung onto the floor. I laughed at the steward till I was bad. He's an old chronic grumbler and gives me many a laugh.

Sunday morning 17th December

The gale died out during the night and the sea has quite gone down. 11am – a fair wind at last but very light. Thank God for it. 6pm – the wind has freshened rapidly, and we soon make eight knots per hour, pass The Brothers Rock and lighthouse[27], sail through the narrow part of the straits and are rounded up in front of the harbour mouth. The fair wind up the straits is, however, a head wind from the harbour and we can't get in! The pilot and four men have come aboard. How strange to see fresh faces!

---

[27] A traditional English-style lighthouse first shone its beam from The Brothers in 1877, fewer than twenty years before Will's voyage.

The tug put off to tow us in, but the captain would not accept the terms and we were all grieved to see her 'Right about!' and make for port, leaving us close to some dangerous reefs and unable to make the harbour. Wellington is called 'Windy Wellington'. Fierce winds prevail for days together and, if the sky be any sign, we are in for a blow for a few days. We may be driven out to sea in the morning. I have asked eagerly for English news from the pilot and stayed talking on deck until 11pm, talking over the news. At 12pm we lay to under a great cliff to rest the men after working the ship hour after hour. I turned in but at 3am was up again as the wind had moderated and we were going to try to tack into the harbour. It is only a mile wide where we are, and only 8 or 9 cables in one place with many rocks about, so that it will require good seamanship and hard work, for the sails will have to be swung around every few minutes to tack and tack.

Monday 18th December

2pm. In harbour at last and anchored in the outer anchorage until the doctor has been aboard and the tug comes to take us alongside. Quite calm now! The whole harbour is surrounded by immense hills resting pile upon pile and Wellington lies scattered on the hills at one end. It all looks very beautiful in the 'glorious sunshine'.

4pm. The doctor has come, and I am going on deck to get passed. He just sees that there is no infectious disease and releases you immediately.

Tuesday 19th December

When the boat left with the doctor and our captain on board to go ashore, we went below when we heard a shout to ask would we like to go ashore, and I hastened like mad and in a moment had sprung over the taff-rail into the boat. The doctor's daughter was there. How delighted I was to see a woman. I could barely keep from rudely staring. She looked so nice! We landed and I immediately procured my letters, but could not send a telegram for reasons which you can guess. I had come away in too great a hurry, but as I expected the tug to bring the ship to the wharf in the afternoon or evening, I did not trouble, but dropped into an eating house for a cup of cocoa to read my letters. How glad I was. I did not know which to open first. My joy was soon damped as poor old Jack Harrison had had none, and I looked up and saw the tears trickling down his face, and if it would have helped him, I would have gladly had less myself that he may have had a few. I cheered him up though as well as I could. I devoured all your letters at once.

I could have cried about poor Harry's wife. My heart aches for him. We afterwards had a walk around, and from many a vantage point looked anxiously to see the old ship coming alongside, but there she lay, and night came on and we ashore and unable to get to the ship. We enquired about beds, but the prices frightened us and at length we engaged a boat, and there was your son rowing in the moonlight across the harbour in a little boat, which danced on every wave and shipped some water too.

The owner sat in the bow. I pulled and Jack steered, and having the tide with us, we soon made the ship (about a mile and a half from shore) and clambered up a rope aboard. Being very tired I soon slept. It was intensely hot or seemed so after being at sea, and my face is burned terribly. Everything looks very queer to an Englishman. The houses are all wood and covered with corrugated iron roofs. They all have verandas and geraniums 12 or 15 feet high growing up them on trelliswork. I only saw one brick building. Government House is built of wood entirely and is the largest wooden building in the world. The streets are wide but full of holes, and far from equal to the worst of country high roads in England. The girls dress very fashionably and awfully stylish, while they have a horribly conceited and independent air! The houses creep up the sides of the hills and many streets are very hilly.

Tuesday afternoon

The captain stayed ashore all night, and only came on board at about dinner time today, and with him brought fresh meat and vegetables. How I enjoyed them at dinner today after tasting none for 13 weeks. Of course, we had to stay on the ship until we were towed ashore, which was not until 3pm this afternoon. I was longing to wire you but was eased when the captain said that he had wired the owners and Gracie Beasley of our safety, and all well, and that it would be in Liverpool papers on Monday night and Tuesday morning. He said it was madness for me to waste money on a wire, but after promising, I am afraid that you will think that there is something wrong, or that I am ill if I do not wire, and would rather go penniless than let you be troubled, and so shall wire.

Tuesday evening

We went ashore about 4pm and went to telegraph as arranged with Mrs Colegate, but they would not take the address as we arranged it, simply 'Coalgate, Liverpool': SAFE. By adding 'Via Eastern Telegraph Co', we thought it would go to the Eastern Office and then, as the Superintendent knows Mrs C at Liverpool, she would get it, but he would not take the address, her not being registered, and I found it would cost me over £2 to wire. I had nothing to say but 'safe'. I could not tell you how I was in a telegram and, on account of the delay of yesterday, the safety of the ship would be published in England by the owners before my telegram landed, so that I reluctantly gave it up. I know I shall worry about you now because I am afraid you will be expecting one and, not getting one, think I am ill. But everything here is terribly dear indeed, and I have heard nothing from James Gough[28].

The depression in Australia[29] has caused hundreds to flock here by every boat, and work is very scarce so that I really cannot spend £2 on a telegram. It would be real madness on my part, for even if I go to Greendale it will cost me a lot, and I may be a long time out of work, for I cannot do anything heavy as although better, I am still weak. I think I am on the right way to recover now and have an uphill start – thank God. Two pounds is a lot even if I were rich, and much as I would give to ease your mind and ease my own about you too, I think that even if I add to your suspense by sending you word by letter instead of wire, you will forgive me and not blame me.

Lodgings are fearfully dear. I have to give the steward at least a sovereign, and without great care by dipping my hands into my pocket for everything, I shall be penniless. You will learn of the safety of the ship, and I hope and trust you will not worry about receiving a telegram. I assure you it worries me, and I wish I had not told Mrs C I would send one. I cannot indeed spend £2 on one. I cannot indeed! I must husband my every penny; I feel the value of it all here. I am sure you will all agree with me when you read this. I have seen Mr Milward, but he holds out no hope for some time, but will do his best.

I am writing to Mr Gough but if I receive no answer shall not thrust myself on him, but consider I am not wanted. God bless you all, and may you be easy in mind and not misunderstand my action in not writing. I would if I could.

---

[28] Will's uncle, through whom he hoped to gain lodgings and employment.

[29] The Australian economy was hit hard following a banking crisis in 1893. The collapse of a speculative property boom in combination with a major international depression led to the collapse or suspension of eleven commercial banks.

I don't care for the £2 but am looking to the future and must take care. I am far from home and among strangers, and they will do nothing for me when the little I have has gone and the £2 would make a big hole in it. I would not have minded the 15 shillings we thought it would cost, but £2 is out of the question. Harrison told his people not to write him until they heard from him as he might leave Wellington the day he arrived, and he never thought of telling them to write to the post office here, so ill as he is with consumption, they won't hear from him for 5 months in all, and his mother was very anxious before he left. They have no satisfaction, so that they have more suspense than you. Poor people never do wire, and I do know Father won't blame me. Had I thought of Mrs C getting to know of our safety from the wires, I should not have thought of wiring. I hope you will conclude that I find it too expensive and not worry.

Wednesday 20th December

I have made my mind up to go to Greendale[30] today and see how they all are. If I do not receive a welcome, I shall not stay. I am going to Lyttelton by the steamer 'Rotorua' (a very small one) leaving at 4 pm today. Fare is 25 shillings and then 6/5d to Kirwee, the nearest station to Greendale.

Saturday 23rd December

I arrived at Lyttelton on Thursday morning. It is no larger than an English village. We were berthed in a cabin for 4, fully occupied and so close and hot that I could not sleep, and like many more spent the whole night on deck.

---

[30] A small farming community on the plains 14km south-west of Hororata, where Will's uncle was a major landowner and farmer. It was named by William White, a partner of James Gough, in memory of his birthplace in Devonshire, England. Established on the previously unidentified Greendale Fault, the strongest earthquake ever recorded in New Zealand was recorded there on 4 September 2010. Five months later, it was superseded by the Christchurch earthquake.

It was beautifully warm and moonlit. The people are very easy in manner. A gentleman Maori, son of one of the members of the House of Representatives, offered me a share in his cabin and in the morning when we parted gave me his address and asked me to visit him on his sheep station in a few weeks, when he would give me many curiosities. I also had an invite to Dunedin, and an Englishman who had come here for his health asked me to go down into Otago with him to a sheep station. He said he knew no one when he came here, but having got an invitation to a sheep owner upcountry, he had made friends and now didn't know which way to go to fill up his invites.

In the towns they are as exclusive as the English, but upcountry very hospitable. I made enquiry in Christchurch, which is a small but pretty place, and everybody seemed to know Mr Gough, who it seems went down to Christchurch very often. I found that the nearest station was Kirwee, from which Mr Gough lived distant 5 miles. There was no train before 4pm and it took 1 hour and 35 minutes to do 30 miles. However I went, and expected to see Mr Gough or one of his men, who I had been told always meets the train for his mail. Kirwee is only a place of small size, 5 or 6 wooden houses, a little wooden station and a country hotel! Mr Gough was not there or any of his men, but I met an Irishman, who quickly said that if I were a friend of Mr Gough's, he would take me any distance. So I clambered up, we fetched my two boxes, and reached Mr G's about 7pm.

We were coming through his land for 3 miles. The country is flat as a table, no trees and only gorse hedges planted on raised banks. It makes a fence in 3 years and keeps the sheep in bounds. You can tell where a man dwells for you can see a group of gum trees and spruce and pine trees growing thick to the bottom, and inside that is a wooden house. These are planted for shelter against the strong winds which often blow. Otherwise, the country is quite open for miles and miles, right up to the mountains. We passed several such houses and my Irish friend said they belong to Mr Gough, and he had several herdsmen living in them. He also told me that he had about 6,000 to 7,000 acres of land and that he lived in his house at this end, and his daughter at the other end. The latter one was the first house he put up after settling. (It is at Greendale, but about 7 miles from here).

At last I reached a large clump of trees and saw a long, low wooden house with bedrooms, sitting rooms and kitchens on the ground floor, and a veranda stretching right round (all the houses have verandas), and a young girl in front who soon ran in. Then a gentleman came out (Mr G), and another who turned out to be Mr Lloyd of Great Ness, who farms about 1,200 acres about 50 miles from here, and had driven over to see Mr Gough. His daughter was also with him. I had a hearty welcome and tears came in both their eyes at seeing one from the Old Country. It seems that Mr Gough sent a letter to Wellington about a month ago, but I never got it, and he was hourly expecting me and had prevailed upon Mr Lloyd to wait in the hope of seeing me. He was very much hurt that I had not received his letter on landing and has since sent for it, but letters here are always much less regular than at home and often lost.

His daughter is married to a Devonshire man named Germain and has 6 or 7 children. Mary's three children live with him and are a great credit to him. The one daughter was down at Greendale, but Ramsay (the young man) and Annie were here. Annie is very pretty and quite accomplished.[31] Ramsay is about 21 and very much like Teddy Lockett in manner and appearance. He is well educated and must be of great service to his uncle, who is quite the gentleman in manner and tone.

---

[31] Will was so taken with Annie that he married her, and they eloped back to Liverpool in England. Sadly, Annie died when their daughter, Millie, was still an infant. In 1899, he married Kate Powell in Bury, Lancashire.

Mr Gough is well read and reminds me of Mr Rogers[32] in his many-sided abilities to talk on so many topics. He (Mr Rogers) must have been a wonderful man. Uncle looks 10 years younger than Father, is active and strong, and rides all over the place amongst the sheep, often going to Christchurch. He has all the influence for many miles round here, sharing it with Sir John Hall[33] (a former premier of New Zealand) who has a large sheep station about 30 miles away. He is the 'moral image' of Uncle Tom and a thorough Gough in appearance and way, being extremely kind.

Yesterday we went to some sport (racing and cycling) at Kirwee. (Mrs G and Sir John Hall were judges). I drove one of the traps with Annie, and we met Mrs Germain (his daughter), her husband and another child of Mary Gough (a young woman of 20), and many more I cannot remember...I was deluged with invitations. Only about 150 people were there, many of whom had come 20 or 30 miles, a distance they think as little of here as you do of three. Mr Lloyd returned to the Greendale end of Mr G's estate at night to proceed from thence to his home this morning. We had a long talk about the Old Country. I like him very much and have promised to ride over on horseback to see him for a few days. I believe there is a big river to ford, but I don't fear that if others have done it. This morning at breakfast, I spoke about my anxiety about you worrying at having no telegram and Mr G said I must not let you stay 5 or 6 weeks more to hear from me personally and he would pay for the telegram. I thanked him and said, No – if I sent it, I would pay for it, and he drove me to Kirwee from where I sent a telegram. It cost me 30 shillings but if it will add

---

[32] No relative so far as I am aware!

[33] Sir John Hall brought the petition for Women's Suffrage before the New Zealand Parliament in August 1893. Hannah Gough was a signatory of the petition. For her relation to the family, see footnote on p.100.

to your comfort, I don't mind. I believe he went afterwards and added my name, which I had left out, concluding that Mrs C would know from whom it came. We afterwards drove round Greendale and saw his other place and the cemetery (only about 12 graves in it) where Mrs C Gough was buried. His eldest daughter aged 20 was married the day before I arrived. I send you a cutting from the paper about it.

I weighed myself here and found I had increased my weight about 14 lbs, so I have done good by coming out. I am so glad! Employment is very hard to get here, but if I can only keep on until this indigestion quite goes and get quite strong, then I do not fear here or home. I knew I looked wonderfully better but was not prepared for such improvement in weight. I feel happier now the telegram has gone for you will know for Xmas Day and as Mr Gough had said, as I had said I would wire, you might easily worry if I were ill or had been washed overboard. He insisted on me sending as it was much too long to wait from 1st Sept to Jan 31st without hearing a word.

I have just eaten two apples Mr Gough has brought me in. Fancy! Ripened in what would be June at home. We are all going over to Greendale on Xmas Day. It does not seem much like Xmas to me at all, and my heart will be with you all at home.

Tuesday 26th December

Xmas Day has come and gone. I write this at 9 am on Monday morning. As we are 12 hours before you, you are all sitting round the fire and perhaps talking and thinking of me. I do hope you have had a happy Xmas and are all well. I have had a much happier Xmas than I expected, although it has been much dampened by thoughts of Harrison, all alone in Wellington. I got quite fond of him having no other society on board, and he cried when I left him at Wellington and was terribly homesick. On Sunday Uncle went over from here to Greendale and Sissy (Mary's daughter) and Lizzie and Jenny and Kate, together with Mr Jasmin's nephew from Christchurch, came over here for the day. Another young man came over on horseback before dinner. They drop in at any time here in this country and tramps are even supplied with a bed and food for two or three days. They never lock the doors when they leave the house as everyone is supposed to be honest. The last three girls I mentioned are half-sisters to Ramsey and Annie and Sissie (Mary's children).

It seems Mary Gough married a man named Hutchison and died, leaving three children whom James Gough took[34]. This Hutchison married again, and after a time his wife died, leaving three more – Kate, Jenny and Lizzie. He then took to drinking and also died, so that these three children are orphans. They have not a relative in New Zealand as their father and mother were English, so Uncle James, as they call him, has them at school, and they make their home at Greendale. It shows the wonderful goodness of the man to father so many who have no claim on him. He seems wonderfully beloved by them all.

We were sitting in the parlour on Sunday night when Ramsay produced his violin, and they began to sing Christmas carols. I cannot believe it is Christmas. Nothing looks like it, but the hymns made me realise it and carried me back to England in thought and I was forced to get up and go out. They told me afterwards they guessed why I went out, and that the Jasmins were the same for a Xmas or two and could not bear to hear the old hymns. They went to Greendale at 8 o'clock, and Mr Gough returned here.

---

[34] Coincidentally, one of Gough's sons – Edwin? – married Hannah Reveley [who signed the suffragette petition] and then died, leaving her with three children. Hannah's sister Ruth Bryden then supported Hannah and the children.

Yesterday morning, Mr Gough and Annie and I drove over to Greendale, and Ramsay rode over for Xmas Day. There were about twenty of us for dinner. They set fire to the Xmas pudding, in which sixpences, threepenny bits, thimbles and buttons were placed for luck. I got none in my bit of pudding. After dinner, a Xmas tree was rigged up on the lawn and the youngsters raced for tops, knives and bags of sweets which Uncle loaded it with and made them race for until they were all gone.

At half past three, I and Uncle (I call him Uncle like everyone else) drove over to Mrs Charles Gough's place about three and a half miles away (Greendale is a district extending for miles), but they were going for a drive. She has a nice place, I can tell you. I saw the presents her daughter had and had to listen to a long tale of the wedding and how she broke down and was ill. She is one of these terribly fussy women and I don't think there is much love lost between her and her brother-in-law. She has three girls and a boy all short and thick. They followed us in a dray and two horses to Mrs Jasmin's and we all had tea together when they left. She invited me to go there for a week or two, but I don't think I shall. She is much more fussy, faddy and stylish than these lot are.

After tea we had a game of rounders and then sang and came then home. As we drove along the roads, no sound of bells met my ears. All seemed so lonely with the houses miles apart and my thoughts went back to you all. It was 10 o'clock on Sunday evening with you. I was hoping you had heard from me by telegram and so were comfortable. They have all been the very essence of kindness to me here. I must thank God for such kind friends. I find the fresh meat and the beautiful butter better for me than the ship's diet, and I hope to keep improving now from day to day. It will take me a long time to get strong if I have the best of luck.

Mr Jasmin who married Mr Gough's daughter (a little homely, and very nice body) came out here many years ago, and his brother followed him about four years ago, and Mr Gough got him a place as inspector of slaughterhouses in Christchurch with £230 per year. There were many applicants, but Mr Gough's influence got it! Wasn't it a grand thing for him! Of course, the one who married Uncle's daughter lives at Greendale and manages his farm of 1,600 acres. He says it is very difficult to get such places or any work suitable for me, but if anything turns up, we are going to have a good try.

There is very little prospect on the land now. It is dear and all taken up where valuable. The men employed on it work very hard, much harder than I shall ever have strength for, and they have to be able to drive a machine, shear or do anything and thoroughly understand about sheep as they rear and breed them here. Uncle has four or six married men in cottages getting £80 per year, and a cow and a horse, and a big garden, and a great many single men who get £1 or 25 shillings per week, and their keep. I hear that it is ten times worse to get work here than at home unless you are a first-class farmhand, and there is no demand for them now as so many have flocked over from Australia.

It is possible sometimes by influence to get a berth and Uncle is going to do his best for me, so I must hope and pray for the best. In any case, I am glad I made a friend of Mr Proctor whom, if I am compelled to return to England, I shall ask to give me some employment. I am sure he will if only at enough to give me a start as he seemed much interested in me, but as this is a very hectic country, I shall do my best to get something here, and in the meantime, I am in good hands, and you need not fret or worry about me in any way.

I wish poor Harrison could say the same, poor fellow! My heart aches for him when I think of him alone in Wellington without friend of any kind. I must write him today to cheer him up. Uncle will take these to Christchurch in the morning and post them. I was about to send them from Wellington on landing, by mail leaving on the 21st, but they told me the 'Frisco mail' on the 28th would get home first, and as that gave me more time I waited to get settled here before sending this. I don't know whether I can get time to let Edwin have a letter this mail, but as he will read this, he must look out for one by next mail if he didn't get one by this. I cannot write to you all at once but will do so as soon as these Xmas holidays are over. They make a lot of Xmas here, and have a whole week of it.

You must address my letters thus: Mr W. Powell c/o Mr J. Gough, Kirwee, Canterbury, New Zealand. Otherwise, they go to Greendale and it is seven miles to fetch them. I hope you will write me as soon as you get this and then write me every two or three weeks afterwards. I shall long for the letter very much. You have all got each other. My eyes blind with tears when I think of you, but it does not do to think of home at all, so I must look at the present and then the future. I am very cheerful except when the indigestion brings on gloominess, and then I fight it off as soon as I can. I shall try to get something to do as soon possible. Employment keeps the mind occupied and free from brooding. If I can't, I shall get a promise from Mr Proctor for work or else go to the Argentine to job. But there is plenty of time yet before I am strong, and I must keep hopeful. I was very glad to get your letters at Wellington but had to pay 5 pennies on Aggie's. Of course, I prefer the letter to the 5 pence, but can't afford it too often.

Well, dear Father and Mother and brother and sisters, you must take this book for a letter and show it to each other. I am so glad to report so much good from the voyage. I can tell you that 14 lbs in my weight have made my face look different, so that despite all the discomforts of a long voyage which I have quite forgotten – I thank God I came. I shall never be a strong man now for two or three reasons, but if I had only come five years ago, before all these years of weakness had impaired my constitution, I might have been as strong as ever. I regret now that I did not. I shall do my best to keep pulling up now. I hope Father is better and I do hope you don't know how much that I may live to see you all again. The thought that anything should happen to you would be too much for me.

I am anxious now to get employment and that is why I have broached it with Mr Gough so soon and then if I do, I shall not come home for four or five years and then only for a holiday. They all go home here every few years. I hope you will not forget Mrs Colegate, and that you will make a close friend of her for my sake, and for all her goodness to me. Should I be fortunate, I shall never know how to repay her.

If you see Lady Mary, you might get a letter to Mr Bush for me. I may come in if I am unsuccessful here, but I leave it to your own judgement. If Mr Gough can't hear of anything, I am afraid my chances are poor as it is several hundred miles to Auckland, and I shan't spend money to go there. I shall write you again in a fortnight to tell you how I get on, and also write to Edwin, Polly and all. Thank him very much for his goodness and kindness. I shall not say how much I shall be glad of a paper. I have a short diary for Mrs Colegate, so you need not send her this. Mr Gough sends his kind regards, and so do your second cousins.

Goodbye. Don't worry about me at all. I shall make my way now, I think, and at any rate I have a better chance than at home, for I am better and stronger and am fit for light work. Whereas when I left England, I was fit for nothing.

Write me soon as you can. God bless and keep you all. With my fondest love to each of you, believe me to remain,

Your loving son – Will

What Happened Next
1894–1899

Will and Annie Gough fell in love, and declared their intention to get married. Annie's parents forbade it on the grounds that they were first cousins. Undeterred, the pair decided to elope, and headed for Wellington, to take ship to England.

One of the parents, we do not know which, pursued them with a wedding present – a beautiful beaver rug – which Will and Kate's daughter Barbara remembered seeing on the double bed at Wigton Hall thirty years later.

Will and Annie returned to England, where Will started a business with a partner. Annie gave birth to two children, the eldest of whom was Millie. The second child was born blind and died shortly afterwards. The doctor stated that the blindness was due to 'consanguinity' as a result of having been born to first cousins, confirming the fears of Mr and Mrs Gough. Will's daughter by his marriage to his second wife, Kate, thought it more likely to have been due to the fact that when the child was born, Annie was already suffering from tuberculosis.

Many years later, Will told Barbara that he had called in a specialist, who arrived with the family doctor. He remembered standing on the stairs and overhearing the specialist tell the doctor, 'He has killed that beautiful girl by keeping her shut up in a warm room with no fresh air!' Annie died shortly afterwards.

To make matters worse, Will's business partner took money from the business and disappeared, leaving behind his wife, two children, and his grieving partner, with a failed business and child of his own to care for.

With the business in ruins, Will took a job with Horners Creamery in Newcastle upon Tyne, the largest suppliers of cream in the country. His job was to source cream and preservatives for the firm, much of which came from farms in Cheshire and Lancashire. One of the farms he visited on a regular basis was run by the Percival family at Harper Fold Farm in Radcliffe, between Bury and Bolton. It was there that he first set eyes on Kate.

Kate was born in 1878 at Parkside Farm, Aston-in-Sutton, Cheshire, close by the River Weaver. The Percivals were a fifth-generation farming family, with 400 acres of land. The grandparents also owned Old Farm and The Dairy Farm in nearby Appleton.

The Percival family, circa 1897
Kate is standing next to her father on the back row

Parkside Farm was extremely successful. During Kate's time there, it won the prize for Best Farm in England. Kate's father, George, took responsibility for the buying and selling, leaving his brother John to the day-to-day running of the farm. At the height of the farm's prosperity, over fifty Irishmen worked on the farm, in addition to a blacksmith, a shepherd and a joiner. Annual auctions of the pedigree stock were held at the farm.

Kate's Uncle Thomas,
a stockman on the farm

During the 1890s, however, two disasters befell the farm. On 4th March 1890, Kate's father, George, together with his cowman, George Percival, visited one of the shippons to tend to an ailing pedigree cow. Having administered gruel, and satisfied themselves that the cow was comfortable, they visited other outbuildings to check on the sheep and newborn lambs. All being well, they retired to bed. The following is a summary of an account from a newspaper at that time:

At four o'clock in the morning the ploughman, Thomas Massey, woke them with the news that two of the buildings were ablaze. Through the heroic efforts of everyone in the farmhouse, all of the boarding employees, three local policemen, and the fire brigade that arrived at 6.30am, seventy cows, thirteen horses, and ten sheep were rescued, together with a number of chickens, and other fowls.

By the time the fire-brigade ceased their exertions, eight cows, eight horses, more than ninety pigs, a hundred hens and ducks, and five sheep, had been roasted alive. In addition, three other buildings were destroyed together with their contents, including three hundred tons of hay and straw, seed oats, seed potatoes, cattle corn, cotton seed, meal, two lorries, a threshing machine and its engine, and scores of farm implements.

The damage was estimated at £3,000, equivalent to £400,000 in 2020. All of this, with the exception of the sheep, was covered by insurance. One can only begin to imagine the emotional impact on the Percivals, and the amount of effort and lost income involved in rebuilding the farm.

But there was more to come. Hard on the heels of the fire came an outbreak of anthrax. The milk had to be tipped away, and all of the animals had to be buried in pits filled with quicklime. No stock could be sold for six months, and even when the restrictions were lifted, none of the other farmers were prepared to risk buying stock from the farm. At this time farmers were not compensated for loss resulting from anthrax. The Percivals were ruined. Things often coming in threes, Kate's grandmother, matriarch of the family, died shortly afterwards.

George decided that they had no option but to move and start again. George's brother-in-law, Ralph, and another uncle, Dan, lent George money to help them get started. They moved twenty-two miles away, to Harper Fold Farm, Radcliffe, midway between Bolton and Bury, in neighbouring Lancashire.[35]

Such was the success that the Percivals made of the new farm that by the time Will Powell came calling, Kate, who was twenty years of age, had opened a restaurant called 'The Creamery' in the Bolton Victorian Market, using money lent to her by her mother.

Will told two of his daughters, Nancy and Barbara, that he had first set eyes on their mother Kate while at Harper Fold Farm, talking to her brother. Will was thirty years of age; Kate was twenty and exceptionally pretty. Will later said that he had walked over to see if she was wearing a ring. When he saw that she was not, he instantly determined to marry her. Will was invited to stay to tea.

After Will had left that night, Kate's mother was reputed to have said, 'Kate will marry that man.' There was, however, one condition. He had to become his own master because, she said, 'We do not marry other people's employees.'

Will swiftly took the hint, and instead of working as an employee of Horners, he set up an agency in Newcastle, selling their products and those of other firms. He and Kate were duly married on 12th April 1899 at the Church of St Thomas, Radcliffe.

---

[35] In 1966, Parkside Farm was owned by Alan Percival, one of Kate's cousins.

Will & Kate
1899–1940

Kate Percival, aged nineteen

Kate and Will's first home, together with Will's daughter
Millie, was at Waverley Cottage, Low Fell, Gateshead.
Will made all of the furniture, and over time they added
antiques, for which they both shared a passion.

From the left: Will, Kate, Dorothy, Bill and Millie,
circa 1909

It was clear from the outset that Will and Kate possessed entrepreneurial spirit. Among the businesses that Will set up were an antiques shop in Northumberland Street, Newcastle, and a classy motor agency, in both of which he installed a manager. He also extended his cream agency into a food company – Powell's Products.

At the age of fifty-two, shortly after the end of the 1914–18 war, Will's health suddenly deteriorated to such an extent that the doctor gave him six months to live. Kate seized the initiative. She sold their house, which at this point was Elmfield Lodge in Gosforth, packed up all their essential belongings in thirty packing cases, and took the family to Fifeshire, where Kate moved herself and the children into a hotel, and installed Will in a hydropathic facility. Millie's husband Harry and Will's brother Fred were left to run the company.

The gamble worked. Will regained his strength and went to join his wife and children for a few months. While in Scotland, Will and Kate hunted for a new home.

They discovered Wigton Hall in Wigton, Allerdale, in Cumbria, nine miles south-west of Carlisle.

Wigton suited their pretensions perfectly. A fine two-storey house dating from the early nineteenth century, it had eight bays in the Gothic Revival style, and three wings forming a U-shape around a courtyard. The front wing was built of glorious golden sandstone, with a battlement parapet with quatrefoil openings, and a green slate roof. The huge two-storey gabled porch had oak doors with tracery panels set in a pointed arch.

The house and grounds had been much neglected, although the interior was beautifully decorated by Waring & Gillow, the famous furniture makers. Of special attraction to Kate was the fact that all of the adjacent farmlands came with the house .

For two days every week, Will travelled over to the north-east to check on his businesses in Gateshead and Newcastle. Unfortunately, sales of both motor cars and antiques struggled in the post-war depression. To make matters worse, the Government had imposed an excess profits tax based on an estimate of the profits that businesses had made before the war. Unable to meet his debts, Will was forced to let both the antiques business and the motor company go. In the garage at the time, for safekeeping, as well as to hide it from the taxman, was a beautiful white saloon belonging to a friend – Mr Scott – who had himself been declared bankrupt.

Will managed to hang on to Powell's Products, and the mortgage on Kate's restaurant, 'Carrick's', because they suspected that the property on which it stood would grow in value, which it did. Their son Bill eventually sold the property to provide an annuity for his mother in her later days.

This was a difficult time for Will and Kate with four children still living at home, and with school fees to pay.

With money left by her brother John, who had recently died at the age of forty-two, following an infection contracted in Africa, Kate erected two huge greenhouses against the old peach wall, in which she produced for sale to the local shops, hundreds of boxes of cress, tomatoes, and other vegetables. She also planted hundreds of raspberry canes.

Will busied himself renovating the Hall and restored one of the wings. Taking advantage of Kate's experience on the Parkside and Harper Fold Farms, they also purchased some Black Galloway and Shorthorn Cross cattle, which they grazed on the twenty-six acres of land.

Throughout this period, which included the Great Depression, the returns from the factory in Gateshead continued to be meagre, and the family depended almost entirely on the sale of their produce. This was not helped by the fact that both Kate and Will believed in 'keeping up appearances', and so Will had mortgages on all of his properties and maintained an enormous overdraft until he was seventy years of age.

Many of their personal antiques, as well as those that had come with the purchase of Wigton Hall, had to be sold off to keep the factory going. Will carried out many of the repairs and all of the joinery in the renovation of the Hall. Kate stitched together strips of old carpet to form new runners for the great landing, and made all her own clothes with the help of a 'sewing woman'.

Throughout this period, much of Kate's attention was devoted to ensuring that their children – apart from Millie who was now married – had a good education. And not just her own children. Kate had been a suffragette during her teenage years, and was outraged when she discovered that the daughter of the sewing woman, having won a place at the Thomlinson' Grammar school for Girls [36], had been refused entry on the grounds that she could not afford the specified uniform.

Kate went up to the Education Department for the county, and demanded audience with the headmistress.

---

[36] Established in 1899 in Westmorland House, Wigton, on the site of what is now the Thomlinson Junior School.

Discovering that only one girl had ever obtained matriculation, despite the headmistress having attended Girton College, Oxford, Kate concluded that the headmistress set greater store by uniforms than scholarship, and promptly withdrew her own children – Nancy and Barbara – from the school. For two years they were tutored by a maths teacher from the boy's school, along with their elder sister Dorothy. When the headmistress was replaced, the girls returned to the school, where they matriculated, and Barbara achieved a distinction.

Dorothy had been an exceptional pupil at Newcastle High School, and the headmistress wanted her to take up a scholarship to Girton College. Kate wept when Will decided they could not afford the remainder of the costs at the same time as having to support the younger children. Dorothy opted to study at the Harper Adams Agricultural College in Shropshire, where she was later given a place on the staff. Determined that the rest of the children should not be denied such opportunities, Kate arranged for Bill to board at the Bootham School and Barbara at The Mount School, both in York and run by Quakers, where they studied for their Higher Certificates. Barbara and Nancy were also sent on an exchange scheme to Germany in the months before finishing school.

The Powell fortunes must have improved around this time, enough at least to enable Will to take out another mortgage, because with Barbara at Girton, they let out Wigton Hall to tenants, and purchased a house in Cambridge at 181 Huntingdon Road, the former home of an Arctic explorer.

This was a happy time. All of the children had studied music, and Kate had learned the piano as a child, and played in the Victorian style on the grand piano in the drawing room. She also had a strong mezzo-soprano voice. A musically talented Jewish undergraduate with lots of records and an Aston Martin car was a frequent guest at the house, and Kate's sister, Marie Hurst, often came to stay at weekends, as did a young man – Sydney Aston – who had grown up with Bill and the girls when they lived at Wigton Hall, and was now articled at a law firm in London. The house was full of music and laughter. There were regular picnics, enlivened by records played on a portable gramophone.

Kate began to attend Cambridge University lectures open to the public and taught herself French. This was partly in response to the Powells entertaining the children of a French family – the Jaboulays – with whom they became good friends.

Will and Kate took on a ...very high-class restaurant where all of the waiters wore dinner jackets' for their daughter Dorothy to run. Unfortunately, this proved too great a challenge for her, and in any case the economy suffered a sharp decline in 1938 with the threat of war, and Will's business suffered again. The family were forced to sell 181 Huntingdon Road and move to Atholl Lodge[37] at 74 Storey's Way, which had been subdivided.

Each winter, for the good of Will's health, the Jaboulays lent Will and Kate their new villa, 'Lou Roustidou,' four kilometres east of Sainte Maxime in Provence. Atholl Lodge would be let to tenants, and the children – who by now had all left home – would visit them there. In the two years before war broke out, Will and Kate lived in France all year round.

In the summer of 1939, Will and Kate travelled up to Brittany and stayed in a monastery that took paying guests in St Jacut de la Mer in Brittany. They lived very simply, eating at long wooden tables in the refectory, and Will helped to keep the flower beds and the kitchen garden tidy.

Will, who miraculously appeared to be overdraft-

---

[37] No. 74 Storey's Way is an impressive house built in 1931, using brick, pebbledash and stone. It has a tower topped with an observatory and stands in a prominent position in what is now a conservation area. It was bought by Fitzwilliam College in 1973. Since 1988, it has been the residence of the Master of Fitzwilliam College, Cambridge.

free for the first time in many years, paid for the children and their partners, including Bill and his fiancée Lorna, to join them for the holidays, putting them up in a cheap hotel by the sea.

Barbara recalled walking along the coastal path with a young Canadian who was also staying at the hotel. Their conversation turned to Hitler's Germany. The young man told her that many Jewish emigrés were leaving Germany and on being refused entry by one country after another, some were committing suicide by throwing themselves into the sea. Barbara had, of course, been in Germany on her exchange visit and remembered seeing huge gangs of brown-shirted youths on the streets. Neither of them could have foreseen where all of this was leading, or the way in which it would shortly impact on Will and Kate.

Part 2
Kate Powell's Diary

May–July 1940
The Escape from France

Monday 6th May

This evening after dinner, Will told me that he had decided to retire early to his room. All day there had been telltale signs that his rheumatism had flared up again. The flicker of pain on his face as he eased himself from his chair; his slow, cautious steps, as though afraid that the earth might give way beneath him; the flexing and unflexing of his hands that made my heart ache to take away his pain. But he bore it all bravely, and I knew that he hated to be pitied. We kissed each other goodnight, and I went up to my own room to sit for a while on the tiny balcony, and watch the sun set over the ancient ramparts.

We are so happy, Will and I, in our little rented house here in St Paul de Vence. Provence has long been our favourite place. The climate of the Alpes-Maritimes, the doctor said, would work wonders for his health, and so it has proved. Not just for Will, but for me too. The warmth of the sun caressing our skin, the clean fresh air off the mountains behind us and the sea ahead.

Will said that it was the Mistral that was responsible both for the luminous quality of light and the purity of the air that had attracted so many painters to Provence, and especially here in St Paul.

'She scatters the clouds and clears the skies,' he said, 'and she sweeps away the dust, and the pollution from all of the wood stoves.'

When our dear neighbour, Monsieur Gattaz, a retired language master from Toulon University, complained about the ferocity of the Mistral, howling through the valleys, bending the trees to its will, forcing everyone to batten down the shutters, and bolt the doors, Will responded,

'I assure you, *cher* Charles, that when you've been halfway across the world in a three-master, as have I, and encountered the monstrous gales between the Cape and the Antipodes, you'll perceive the Mistral as nothing more than a gentle breeze!'

This unfailing positivity is one of things that first attracted me to Will – that and his handsome looks, his charming manner, and a wisdom beyond his years.

I said that we are happy and settled in this delightful Saracen fortress town, built on a ridge between two lush valleys. At this time of year, the peasants are reaping a rich harvest of plump violet artichokes – their flowers resembling giant fluffy cornflowers – and baskets full of roses for the perfumeries in Grasse. Everything has the air and appearance of past and future centuries of peace, prosperity and security.

I learned today that Bill, as part of the three months' holiday he has given himself following that wretched illness he had from overwork, is coming to join us here in St Paul. He says that Lorna will follow on as soon as she has received the necessary papers to leave the UK. I cannot wait to see them, and I know that it will be the best tonic that Will could possibly have.

Friday 10th May

I think I may have mentioned Monsieur and Madame Berlioz before? We have only recently become acquainted. They live near us in a delightful house, with a better view than ours, and more open to the sun. This dear man and his wife are very French and very frugal, Mme's costume being of the last period of long, full Basque costume coats, with ground length, very full gored skirt. Monsieur Berlioz's are with very narrow trousers of the same period – no frills about them at all. They have spent several '*vacances*' in England, and love the English. Even going so far as to adopt an English neighbour – Miss Smith – whom they have nursed back to health.

Miss Smith, it transpires, had been turned out of her prosperous business in teas and antiques as the result of the property being bought over her head. The house had overlooked the south-west valley and the Mediterranean, a really a marvellous and unique position on the ramparts. She had built a good terrace and generally improved it with her profits. With the little money she had left after being forced to leave her home, she bought an old wine cellar on the opposite side of the eight-foot street, and had it converted.

The war had commenced and nothing further could be done, and since her friend, a writer, had left, she installed herself in the empty rooms rent-free, with no money. She had lived on wild potatoes, dandelions and next to nothing, until her appetite had failed. She ended up with a breakdown and pneumonia, followed by six months of bronchitis.

When Monsieur and Madame Berlioz first discovered Miss Smith, she was in poor health, with just her dear little pedigree dogs for company. They brought her soup and one apple each day, and prepared a terrace garden for her in their '*propriété*' in the valley so that she could benefit from the sun on her face.

This evening Madame Gattaz burst in, breathless, her face flushed, and her silver hair awry, with the news that they had just heard on their wireless that the Germans have attacked Holland and are advancing towards Belgium and France. She invited Will and I to join her and Monsieur Berlioz tomorrow evening to listen in for further news. We immediately accepted.

After she had left, Will and I wondered what this might mean. Will tried to convince me that there was nothing to fear. That despite all of his bluster and fine speeches, Hitler would find the combined might of the armies of the British and French empires more than he bargained for.

'Besides,' he said, 'we are hundreds of miles away from the action here in our little village. We are completely safe.'

As I write this, I have to say that I am not entirely sure that either of us were truly convinced.

Saturday 11th May

This morning, just as we were about to leave for the bakehouse, there came a knock at the door. A husband and wife from New Zealand were standing there, accompanied by a little girl. He was a writer, and they had come to St Paul for the season. Seeing the 'To Let Furnished' sign over the door, which had not been taken down, he had been hoping to rent our house. I explained that we were here for the duration, and they left in search of an alternative house to rent. They seemed a delightful young couple. I am sure they will find somewhere suitable.

As soon as they were gone, we set off, as I was anxious to get my bread into the oven. The sky was a clear blue, the barometer set fair, and the sun already beginning to take the chill off the cobbles and ancient stone walls. As always, Will came with me, because I hate the steep ladder down to the oven in the cellar.

When we arrived at the baker's, the boulangerie was packed with the familiar mix of locals and foreign residents like ourselves. While Will paid our fifty centimes for the use of the oven and descended the ladder to set my loaf with all of the others, I sat upstairs with some acquaintances.

Having briefly discussed the news of the German advance, our conversation quickly returned to the customary discussion of the meals we had prepared since last we met, and the swapping of recipes. The baker's wife gave me a scrap of paper on which she had written the recipe for *aubergines farcies aux anchois*, that she had promised in return for the one I had given her a fortnight since, of my crispy-topped Cumberland pie. She told me that she had cooked it for herself and her husband and they had thoroughly enjoyed it, even though she had made it with slow-cooked lamb, rather than the feather-blade beef we traditionally use.

In this communal atmosphere I invited Madame Berlioz to come to tea next Sunday, with her husband.

On my way back to the house, I was accosted by Mme Gattaz. Did I know that the Prime Minister Neville Chamberlain had resigned last night, and Mr Churchill had been asked by the King to form a new government? I did not, but it hardly came as a surprise. When I told Will, he expressed doubts about the wisdom of the move.

'Let us hope he handles this situation better than he did the Gallipoli campaign,' he said. 'I am surprised that people have such short memories.'

'In fairness,' I reminded him, 'it is Mr Churchill who has taken the lead in calling for rearmament in the face of rampant German militarism. I am surprised that Mr Chamberlain had such a short memory. Pacification did not work in 1914. How could he have imagined that it might when Hitler has so much support among his people, and Germany such great grievances?'

He took a puff of his cigar.

'Even so,' he replied, 'I am surprised that you have warmed to Mr Churchill, given his opposition to women's suffrage?'

'I can forgive his youthful antipathy to suffrage,' I told him, 'although as members of the Liberal Party, we did expected him to be more enlightened than the rest of the Establishment. However, he did insist that those suffragettes arrested on Black Friday and on other occasions were immediately released. And he did come round to our cause in the end.'

Will chuckled.

'When he realised there were votes in it,' he said.

I knew that that real reason Will had such a down on Mr Churchill was because he blamed him for his decision to return the pound to the gold standard in 1925 at its pre-war parity, for forcing prices down and hitting our businesses so hard.

After tea, Will and I went to our neighbours' house, and huddled around their wireless. We stayed quite some time, as Charles searched between the three French channels before settling on Radio Paris. We learned that a great battle was taking place between the German army and the Dutch army at a place called Grebbeberg – I am not exactly sure of the spelling – close to the border between the two countries. The Germans had made progress, but the Dutch had launched a counter-attack. We also learned that President Roosevelt had banned submarines belonging to what he called 'belligerent nations' from using American ports and territorial waters. Yesterday, we were told, Roosevelt had also frozen assets held in the United States belonging to Belgium, Luxembourg and Holland, to prevent them falling into the hands of the Germans.

'I fancy that he will need to do more than that before this is over,' Will said.

Monday 13th May

After a leisurely breakfast, I suggested that we take a stroll along one of our favourite routes around St Paul. Will agreed, on condition that I did not set too fast a pace.

It was another glorious spring day as we walked slowly up to the Porte de Vence, and into the Place de Jeu de Boules. This early in the season, there were empty tables outside the charming Café de la Place. We ordered two café crèmes and spent a pleasant half an hour watching *les anciennes* standing in the shade of the plane trees, putting the world to rights, and playing hotly disputed games of boules. Or, more accurately, according to Monsieur Gattaz, pétanque – that offshoot of the traditional *jeu Provençal* that has become so popular.

When we could justify sitting here no longer, we headed back up to the imposing fortified gateway of the Porte de Vence, turned right behind the tower, and began to walk south along the ramparts towards the Porte de Nice. Pausing halfway, we leaned on the wall and took in the panorama.

In the gaps between the pines on the slope beneath us, we glimpsed the neat rows of vines on the terraces and admired the vivid green of their bursting buds. On the opposite slopes of the valley, creamy drifts of almond blossom and apple blossom were interspersed with the pale pink of cherry trees. Here and there, among the olive groves, poppies painted the hills scarlet, with a triumphant display that the early summer sun will shortly scorch and wither away.

Every year that we come back, Will and I comment on the number of new properties dotting the foothills to the west. This year, the number seemed to have doubled, their pink-tiled roofs just visible above the hedges of cypress newly planted as protection from the onslaught of the Mistral.

'In another fifty years, it will be possible for a moderately small giant to step from roof to roof all the way from here to the Cap d'Antibes,' Will joked.

I hope he is wrong, even though if he were proved right, neither of us will be here to see it.

We set off again, and strolled on until we left the ramparts, and stepped down to reach the cemetery, just outside the walls. There is something special, I think, about a French cemetery. And the cemetery of St Paul – with its back to the towering walls of the Porte de Nice, and its front facing the azure blue of the Mediterranean Sea, is unique. We entered through the iron gates, guarded by a massive oak and an ancient yew, and were immediately in an oasis of calm and serenity.

The rows of bright white and grey marble – their varied size and height reflecting the relative wealth of the families interred there – are immaculately kept. The plaques are embossed in gold with the names of the dead, some with photographs that fix the loved ones forever in a moment of time. There is a peace and tranquillity about the place that cannot fail to cause one to reflect not only on the impermanence and fragility of life, but also on the debt that every generation owes to those who came before.

We retraced our steps through the Porte, and took the Rue Grande, slowly wending our way uphill, pausing to peer into some of the artist's studios along the way. It quickly became clear that Will was finding difficult the combination of the heat and the slope, and so we turned first into the tiny square, La Placette, encouraged by the refreshing sound of the gushing fountain, and then just around the corner into the Place de la Grande Fontaine, where Will needed no encouragement to splash his face and neck with the chilly mountain water before taking refuge in the cool of the vaulted washhouse.

We sat side by side on one of the stone blocks where the clothes are rubbed and pummelled with soap before being plunged into the cistern. In no time at all, we began to shiver with the shock of the cold in this shadowy retreat and decided to continue on our way.

Turning right onto the steep and aptly named Montée de la Castre, we climbed slowly up to Place De l'Eglise, where we rested for a short while on one of the pews at the back of the Church of the Conversion of St Paul, before descending through narrow winding streets, where several of the houses sport wisteria and jasmine whose scents competed for our attention.

I had no idea how much that short walk had taken out of Will. He immediately went for a lie-down and did not surface until teatime.

The rest had a miraculous effect, and Will was more animated than I had seen him in days. When we arrived at Maison Gattaz, I had several times to tell him to hush because he was distracting Charles who was trying to tune the wireless to the BBC Overseas Service in time for a promised news broadcast.

It was comforting to hear the familiar sound of Alvar Lidell, although Will said he sounded rather like someone commentating on the Derby. We were just in time to catch him introducing a recording of Winston Churchill's speech to Parliament earlier this evening. It was a very short, yet powerful speech in which he committed himself wholeheartedly to the task of defeating the Germans, and saying that he had nothing to offer, '. . . but blood, toil, tears and sweat.' He spoke of '. . . an ordeal of the most grievous kind', and 'many, many long months of struggle and of suffering'.

The response from the Labour Members of the House was resounding, but the Conservative MPs were far more muted. It seemed they still wanted Neville Chamberlain.

When the broadcast was over, Charles turned off the radio. Our mood had changed. There was a most sombre atmosphere in the room. I believe that it was the first time that the full import of what may be ahead dawned upon us.

Wednesday 15th May

This morning, having been informed of the necessity to do so, I went to Nice for a military permit to stay in St Paul. I was sent from bureau to bureau, at each one of which I was assured that I had been misinformed, and a permit was not required.

Having stood in three separate queues, in thundering rain for which I had come unprepared, I was almost drowned. There was nothing for it but to leave without refreshment and hurry for the bus, it being necessary to be there at least half an hour beforehand.

What a surprise when Bill got on the bus! We were so happy to see one another that I quite forgot my wretched appearance. It was now over a fortnight since Nancy had written announcing his departure from Plawsworth and his possible arrival, at the same time that her letter reached us in St Paul. He said he had been about eight days coming, five or six of them at Folkestone waiting to dodge the mines, and later in Paris. He said he had sent me a wire the day before. When we arrived home, Will had it in his hand and waved it at us with a grin from ear to ear.

As soon as we had Bill settled in his room, I immediately went out and bought a shoulder of mutton. I had it boned, beaten and rolled with a long salted sausage, French fashion, and have set it aside for two days before roasting it. Bill joked that it reminded him of the parable of the Good Samaritan and the fatted calf. I told him I hoped that was not because he had been living a life of sin and debauchery while we were away, and Will said he wondered if that explained Bill's need for a good rest?

He exclaimed that chance would be a fine thing, and we all had a good laugh at that.

Despite the news reports, and the disruption to Bill's journey, the war seemed far away and on another plane. We passed a pleasant day catching up with each other's news, talking of buying one of the lovely plots outside the walls for a future home, and basking in the sunshine and the carefree atmosphere.

This evening Bill came with us to Monsieur and Madame Gattaz's house to listen to the broadcasts. How our mood was changed. We learned that the Netherlands surrendered to Germany this morning, and in response to a terrible blitz upon Rotterdam by the Luftwaffe, the RAF have begun bombing cities all over Northern Germany. It immediately put me in mind of Barbara's young man, John Day, the charming South African who came to England to fight for the Empire, and whom Bill tells us is now a pilot officer in an RAF bomber.

Most worrying was the news that the German army has won a great battle at Sedan, has captured all of the bridges over the River Meuse, and is advancing unimpeded towards the English Channel! I could stand no more, and left Will, Charles and Bill deep in conversation to come home and prepare a light supper. Hopefully tomorrow will bring better news.

Thursday 16th May

What a surprise today brought. The French military came up from the next village, filling the narrow street as they went to prearranged billets within the village. Some of them proceeded to wash with oil and soap and shave themselves at the fountain opposite our front door, and then proceeded to wash their shirts. The fountain was a perpetual diversion. They seemed so young and innocent, and completely unaware of their own vulnerability.

On the other side of the house, about sixty feet below us, were their motorcycles and some mules to draw the small guns. None of this seemed to bring the war nearer. I asked an officer with whom we became acquainted what the soldiers talked about, and he said, 'Never the war, but what they would do when demobilized.'

The officer is newly married, and his wife and I spent the afternoon going to Miss Smith's garden to water and replant. Miss Smith, now fully restored to health, is interested in taking up nursing, a full-time occupation, and expensive too, given that she has no money for phone calls and the journeys she must make to seek aid from influential committees. We advised her to go to London, where there was sure to be a shortage of trainee nurses.

I feel sure that she will make an excellent nurse, because on those occasions when Will's rheumatism is so painful that he must sit in a darkened room for hours on end, Miss Smith has proved to be the most efficient and careful giver of injections that I have ever met, and although poor herself, she has been making excellent beef tea for a boy recovering from pneumonia. To all intents and purposes, she is the unpaid district nurse.

Despite our advice and her reduced circumstances, I fear that she has set her heart on staying in St Paul, declaring that if the Italians do make war, she would find plenty to do here for the inhabitants. Claiming that 'one government or another would be the same thing'.

That is all very well, our French officer pointed out, but if Germans do come this far down, or if a deal is done with the Italians, then English persons such as herself – and us, for that matter – might very well be interned, or worse.

We were still discussing this and other matters when Madame Mermoz, our milk-woman – a large peasant who only shouts mongrel French, mostly Italian – told us that she was going tonight into the hills twenty miles nearer the Italian border to bring home her own parents, whose safety she fears greatly.

Hearing this, Miss Smith became extremely anxious on our behalf, saying, 'I feel towards you as to my own parents, and I wish you would leave immediately.'

I went home a little perturbed by this, but on the way met Bill returning from a long walk with Mr Muir, the young New Zealand writer who wished to rent our home, with whom he has made fast friends.

After tea, Will and I decided not to impose on Monsieur and Madame Gattaz this evening. We had all had such a pleasant day we did not wish to spoil it. However, Bill said that we ought to consider acquiring a wireless ourselves, as it was important that we stay in touch with the course of the war, given that we were so far from home.

Wednesday 22nd May

It is five days since my last entry. We hired a wireless ourselves, listening to every rumour and every 'it is said' with a qualm. A great deal has been made by reports of our splendid and brave allies, with the French praising their brave soldiers who were holding the line, always holding the line. We had been taught for years of the invincibility of the French! But the Germans were already in Holland, where the Dutch having held on magnificently, were forced to capitulate, crushed by weight of numbers and treachery.

We felt sooner or later, when met by the concentrated Allied forces, Germany would be retarded, and we should – because of outside communications – be the victor: never a doubt!

This morning, however, Bill became uneasy all at once and prepared for home, going to Nice to enquire about his exit visa. On his return, in between packing his things, he tried to persuade us to go with him in the car to St Malo. The Germans have now commenced their offensive and are making great headway into north-west France. Indeed, only today we learned that a battle has begun for Boulogne, and Calais is under siege. Until now our faith in the unity and strength of the Allies has kept away all fear, and daily we have been expecting to hear of a major check to the German advances. We are beginning to fear that this is simply blind faith. We have not yet given up all hope of staying here in St Paul, but Will and I did agree that it was perhaps wise to at least begin to pack much of our belongings so that we would be ready to leave if needs must.

Saturday 25th May

For the past two days we have packed. This house has been our home, and I had not realised how much we had accumulated. Over the past months we have built up stores of sardines, milk and many other goods, and pots, pans and all the other utensils essential to everyday living.

Yesterday Bill went to Nice to collect his exit visa and was ready to leave. He had hoped that we might leave with him, but we are not quite ready – either in practical terms or in our resolve, and he had to go. His visa, once granted, gives him only eight days' grace to stay in France. He left at lunchtime today. Boulogne having been already bombed, and Dieppe mostly in use by the military, he is heading for Paris en route to Le Havre or St Malo. Although I have not shared this with Will, I know that I will be anxious until I know that he is safe, and back with Lorna, in England.

Now we are living with the bare minimum – that which we have not yet packed – and eking out our dry food store, although there is still plenty of fresh food available in the shops. At least we still have this roof over our heads, and the benefit of a garden, which many do not.

Once Bill had gone, Will and I went to sit in the garden. He puffed on his cigar in the shade, while I took a little sun, and reflected on how lucky we are here in this medieval fortress, surrounded by our military with their mules.

As I write this, however, I have a feeling that we are doped with a false sense of security, and with our bags packed and no decision about where, when, or if we should go, it feels rather like sitting on a fence.

Sunday 26th May

After an excellent meal of roast lamb, tiny new potatoes, asparagus, strawberries and cream, and coffee, we went into the garden as usual.

Although the prices are constantly rising, there is no shortage of food of excellent quality. Beef is no longer available – everything having been killed under six years of age – but there is an unending supply of veal, mutton, lamb and chicken. The price of chicken is much higher than we are used to at home, where it is normally 2/6d a lb, whilst here it is 3/6d. As it is May, pork is cheaper, and I feel that the poor must be eating this meat, as all men in France up to 40 years of age are now serving under the flag. There must be a great many of them who only eat pork.

Our French officer told me that the men at the front line earn the equivalent of 1/5d[38] per day, and behind the line 11d. There is a wife's allowance of 1/6d per week, and each child 1 shilling, with preference given to the wives in government work, and families augmenting the men's allowance by sending parcels.

We hear rumours that prices have soared far beyond the pocket of these soldier's wives and there is much dissatisfaction among them – not feeling that it is worthwhile their husbands fighting for so little.

Our impression is that France remains a land of plenty if one were prepared to pay the price, such as heeling shoes, which has risen from 4d to 9d, washing sheets – three for 2/-. It can only be that there is enormous profiteering going on.

There is still an ample supply of unskilled labour, and we see many efforts of public charity, such as soup kitchens and the washing and repairing of soldiers' uniforms. But life is dear for the less fortunate. Even strawberries grown in the nearby fields under excellent climate conditions and with no transport costs are at this moment 1/- per lb, against 4d two years ago!

Letters are now very late, often taking four to six days from Paris, and two days in transit from street to street in Nice. Other than the unskilled labour I mentioned, there is little or no skilled or professional labour to replace the absentees. This is making for queues everywhere. To make matters worse, in public places and in luxury shops, the ladies of the family chat away to leisured friends or visitors when they should be serving customers. When one does reach the front of the queue, service and attention are just thrown at you. Paper being in short supply, everything is wrapped in old paper or newspapers. Lavatory paper is non-existent

---

[38] This corresponds to one shilling and five pence, or £4.80 in today's money. 11d (11 pence) is equivalent to £3.11 now. 1/6d is now worth £5.08, and 1 shilling is £3.39. Compare this with the cost of meat above.

for the purpose for which it was intended, as it is being used as a matter of course by bakers to wrap around the bread for the purchaser to take the bread from the baker. Today I observed a baker wait until a customer had placed the bread in her reticule, and then pull the paper back so that he might use it again!

Before this war began, there was much eating in the two popular hotels – 6/6d per head – and 7/6d per head in La Colombe d'Or. I was told that St Paul was made very popular in pre-war days by the Aga Khan. The restaurants are still very crowded now for lunches and teas, but only with French people.

What has been a tranquil day ended with the news that our troops, and those of our allies, have been surrounded at Dunkirk and a fierce battle is underway.

Monday 27th May

This morning, while Will and I were leisurely eating breakfast and reading, Mr Muir burst in, breathless from running, saying, 'I feel I must tell you immediately that Leopold[39] is going over to the Germans, and I am going to England today. She needs every able-bodied man.'

This was a stunning blow. I visualised the Allied troops in total defeat; the surrounded in their hundreds and thousands, with all the war equipment. I almost choked from shock, my brain reeling. I found myself repeating over and over again, 'The Devil! The Devil! Oh! The Devil!'

I immediately took Mr Muir to repeat the wireless message to Will in full. He sat there in silence and listened intently without comment – he who is usually so full of chat.

Mr Muir had told us that several months ago he had gone to England from Italy in order to offer himself as a soldier, but been advised to return to New Zealand to

---

[39] King Leopold III of Belgium, who surrendered to the Germans on 28 May 1940 to avoid further bloodshed of his people.

join up. On his return he had intended to stay in Italy to write his romances, but the newspapers were so anti-British, and one newsreel shown at the films was of the terrors and destruction in Poland, finishing with 'So end all enemies of Fascism'. And this was always followed by a relief map of Britain being attacked, and ending in flames and smoke, which made him boil with rage. And so, he and his bride left Italy and came here for a more congenial atmosphere.

And now he has decided that he will return to England in the certain belief that this time his offer will be gratefully received.

I am so glad and proud that our colonial brothers should be so fired up to help us in our dark hour of need and trial.

During the day, the Muirs brought their leftover groceries and said goodbye to the delightful furnished house for which they had paid three months in advance and ate lunch and an early tea with us, before taking a taxi to Antibes to catch the express for Marseilles en route for England.

After they had gone, we tuned into the wireless, and learned that the evacuation of our troops from Dunkirk, under fire, has begun. May God protect them.

Friday 31st May

Over the past four days, we have heard on the wireless and read in the papers of the miracle that is to save France. The covering of our troops and the French army from the air by the brave airmen of the RAF has allowed them to retreat – in order – to the coast, where, by the grace of God, boats of all sorts, shades, shapes and sizes await them.

Close to eight thousand British troops were evacuated on Monday alone, and many more since. We feel proud and secure at this marvellous feat and hope for some really tangible check to stop the dreadful

German progress. The united strength of the two great empires must break them sometime, and we have great hope that this will be so, now that they are under the control of the new French Generalissimo, Maxime Weygand. His name is electric, and everyone is of the opinion that we will now leap to victory.

This newfound confidence has kept Will and I in our beautifully situated apartment, with its terrace hanging in the air over the ramparts, hundreds of feet above the valley, where the peasants go each morning to gather roses for the perfumery. The thought flitted through my head that if the war turns for the worst, they may never become finished merchandise. Then I felt ashamed that I should even contemplate it.

But we are not taking anything for granted. Everything is still packed and Will decided today that it would be better to put it all on the car, because where it is currently stored, it is attracting the flies that are becoming more abundant as the summer approaches. Indeed, the mosquitoes will be emerging soon.

Will also believes that it would be prudent to gather supplies of petrol before it becomes too scarce. He said that it would not be enough simply to fill the tank, because if we should have to flee France altogether, we would not have enough. And so, he has hatched a plan to buy gallon tins and to fill them, and then attach them to the car with our luggage. There are two problems, however. Firstly, it has been declared illegal, in order to prevent hoarding, to fill tins from the pumps. And secondly, all of the pumps have signs saying 'Military only'.

Fortunately, a friend of ours, a local woodcarver, has come up with a solution. He has lent us a piece of rubber tubing to siphon the petrol from the tank in the car into the cans, and he says he knows of someone in Vence who owns some pumps and will be prepared to fill our tank. Will and our friend intend to go in the car to Vence tomorrow while the opportunity still exists.

Where would we be without our French friends?

Saturday 1st June

Early this morning, our friend went with Will to Vence and found someone who was indeed willing to fill our tank. Each time the tank was full, they had to drive the car into the woods where they siphoned petrol into the tins, before returning to the pump and beginning again. This they continued to do until all twelve tins and the car tank were filled, and we had enough for whatever journey we might have to undertake.

All is still very peaceful here in St Paul. Our small shops are full of just fruit and vegetables, and the delicious fresh soft fruit, artichokes, peas and potatoes are cheap and varied. Only one multiple shop is fully stocked with other groceries. Coffee is now a thing of the past but ground and roasted barley is on sale as a substitute, although we are fortunate to still have some bottles of prepared coffee of excellent quality. There is plenty of high-priced meat and, for the not so rich, plenty of pork and prepared ham. And there is no lack of wine of the best vintages, although imported alcohol is now unattainable – Will's favourite, from Berry Brothers of St James, having been the first to be out of stock.

This afternoon we invited our little English friend, Miss Smith, to sit with us in our garden. The sky was devoid of clouds and in the distance, seven or so miles away, we could see the distinctive azure of the Mediterranean. Will explained that it was the absence of decaying plants on the seabed that explained why this was so, when the oceans across which he had travelled as a young man were so green.

Our conversation turned to the power of the new Generalissimo Weygand, and our sense that France has a new impetus and desire to win the war, but that something must be done for their soldiers, as articles are appearing in the papers about the difference between the German soldiers and their own.

There is a new unease, however, regarding the Italians. Mussolini has boasted for so long of his power that the children here have been allowed to finish school three weeks early, in case there should be an invasion. Today was the date he promised to enter the war, but as there has been no sign of him doing so, we are beginning to think it nothing more than bluster. An idle threat.

We walked Miss Smith to her door and, as we turned to go, she said she had a sense of foreboding, and urged us leave St Paul immediately and leave France too.

This evening we listened intently to the news on the wireless. The evacuation from Dunkirk is still underway, with tens of thousands embarking at a time. There has a been a German victory in Nordland, a region of Norway, but no talk of further German advances in France, and still nothing from Mussolini. It is hard to know what to think about whether we should leave or stay.

Monday 3rd June

Yesterday Will and I made a momentous decision. We are leaving our home here in St Paul and moving to Sainte Maxime, via Cannes and Esterel. Will says that it is too early to flee the country entirely until we have a better sense of how things will unfold. Sainte Maxime is somewhere we know well, and is forty-five miles further from the Italian border, and closer to Marseilles and to the Spanish border, which is where he believes that we should head if we do decide to leave altogether.

I cannot say exactly what it was that decided us, but the situation is becoming more desperate in Dunkirk, with the evacuation now taking place only under cover of darkness because of the Stuka attacks on the defenceless men on the beaches. The remaining French forces – the last line of defence – have been pushed back into the town itself. Hitler has been seen on French soil, stomping around the Allied memorials from the last war like a demented savage. And here in the Alpes-

Maritimes, a round-up of all Italians has taken place, due to the growing fear of an impending invasion. Heaven knows who will do all of the work, as here in the South there are few French workers, and approximately sixty-eight percent of the schoolchildren are Italian!

We have spent all day packing our remaining food supply, paying the garage bill for the car, and saying our goodbyes.

We plan to leave early tomorrow morning. I had intended to call first in Nice, where a set of my false teeth are awaiting collection, but our French officer has advised against it, and so I shall have to wait until we are back in England to arrange another set.

I shall feel sad to leave here. It has been our home, on and off, for over three years. We have made good friends – Monsieur and Madame Gattaz, and Miss Smith, to name but a few. Life has been good to us here, and Will's strength and vigour has been so much improved, notwithstanding his ups and downs. But I can see that we must bite the bullet and go. The sooner the better.

Tuesday 4th June

We left at 7 o'clock this morning, and we were not alone.

The roads were choked with vehicles, some with trailers and some without. Piled high on the roofs of cars and vans, light wagons, and horse-drawn vehicles were mattresses, complete with eiderdowns. Dolls and family perambulators were attached with rope or wire to radiators, and luggage grilles hung precariously as the vehicles bounced and swayed ahead of us.

When we arrived in Cannes, the town was in a state of panic. Everything in the shops appeared to be on sale, and people had even set up stalls beside the road. Had we been in the right state of mind, there were many excellent bargains to be made. Will bought two bottles of rum at half price and we decided to take coffee in a popular café that was quite empty. We were not able to stay long as the police arrived to tell us to move on, to enable some of the wider vehicles to pass.

To avoid being jammed in by the traffic, we took the route by Esterel. We travelled at our own pace, every mile bringing contentment to Will, who by now was tired from pulling the steering wheel with his poor rheumatic arms, and from time to time we stopped to stroll along the road and talk of past drives along this stretch, and happy memories of times spent here with the family. When all was calm and we were rested and with hope renewed, we continued our journey.

We made our next call at Sainte Maxime to visit the poste restante and collect some money, Bill having promised to send some from England. There was a postcard from him saying he could not get a boat but hoped to very soon, and he would then arrange for the money to be available from the bank in Sainte Maxime as promised.

The bank being closed, and despite our concern for Bill's safety, we managed to enjoy a picnic lunch under a large plane tree at our favourite café. There were very few people about, and after lunch we went to the bank, where we discovered that the money was in fact at St Raphael where we could elect to go to collect it next day, or sign for a letter of credit to be sent from the bank in St Raphael to here in Sainte Maxime, where we could collect it in three days' time. Will and I both signed, despite the fact that it was painful for him to do so.

The atmosphere here is very calm and peaceful compared with Cannes. We met a lady who had stayed with us here a year before, who is now at Grimaud staying with Scotch friends. She is here for the duration but wants to go home to do something for her country, but does not care to break with her moral obligation to stay with them as she had arranged.

I find Sainte Maxime to be as delightful as of old, and Will is anxious to stay. He has found his Mecca. So I went immediately to the house agent who had supplied us with a property before, and we ran around in the car seeing a number of furnished houses, before deciding that it would be wiser to stay in a hotel for a while. I was told by the hotel manager that permission to stay must be given by the Mairie, and so I went to obtain it.

Imagine my astonishment on being told that evacuees must go to Avignon. I said that we were not evacuees, just tourists. The official was most abrupt, saying we must leave the Alpes-Maritimes immediately!

I was astounded and asked if Dr Feeze, who had been our medical advisor, was still the mayor. Being told yes, I went to his surgery and found him there. He explained that what I had been told was true: part of the regulations introduced because of the war. 'But . . .' he said, '. . . as you have been here regularly during the last three to four years, I will phone the Prefect and tell him to provide you with permission.'

I hurried back to the Mairie and was relieved to discover that a permit was waiting for me with the Mayor's official stamp. I returned to the hotel, where Will had become anxious about my long absence, and we booked a room for the night. After a light supper, Will went straight to bed, exhausted after the long and eventful day. Now that I have finished this entry, I shall go and join him.

Wednesday 5th June

Yesterday we found a nice apartment on the higher ground away from the sea. It is a large, well-built villa in its own sizeable and sheltered garden. We took possession this morning and decided to have a picnic lunch in the valley of Plan de la Tour.

What a wonderful decision it proved to be. This paradise, nestled in the heart of the Massif des Maures, has always been a favourite place for us to come with the children whenever we are in the South of France. The enchanting Provençal village with its church of St Martin, and the little square with its traditional market surrounded by restaurants, shops and bars, is sufficient reason to make the six-mile drive up into the hills from Sainte Maxime. But for Will and for me, the real draw is always the valley itself.

Surrounded by the hazy blue mountains of the Massif, the open plain is a trove of forests, vineyards and fields full of wheat and barley, interspersed with poppies, cornflowers and wildflowers of every hue. On the hills, the *garrigue* is resplendent with golden broom, and the air heady with the scent of wild thyme, rosemary, *Pinus pinea* and umbrella pine.

Will wandered off, leaving me to unpack our picnic lunch. He was gone for some time, and when he returned, he looked the happiest I have seen him since we left St Paul. He told me that he had been paddling in a stream.

We sat on our rugs in the shade of an oak tree, and feasted on chicken legs and a salad of asparagus and new potatoes, with a French dressing I had prepared, all washed down with Perrier water, and the last bottle of our treasured Beaujolais. Then strawberries with a little pot of cream to finish. Replete, we lay on the rug together and dozed off to the sound of a nightingale singing in a nearby hedgerow, a sound that is familiar to us here, even in the daytime.

When we awoke, it was late in the afternoon and the shadows were lengthening. Reluctantly, we packed up and set off.

As we drove home, Will declared that our picnic had been one of the very best, and that we must have many such days.

Thursday 6th June

This morning, Will went into town to look for two very good deckchairs for our better comfort. He returned with a grin on his face, and laughingly said that he had spied nearly a dozen cheap ones that had subsided on one side or the other. He had settled on two that were in better shape and less likely to collapse. He had paid 120 francs for the two.

'But,' he said, 'we shall have many years' pleasure from them. They have labelled them, and I will call for them when they are settled.'

We had tea under the plane tree and exchanged greetings with several residents, including the 'domestic' at Chez Moi, the small villa a short distance outside of the town, near to the shore, where Bill and Lorna spent their honeymoon. She had heard that we were here in Sainte Maxime and came up specially to see us.

After dinner, we went out for a stroll and were accosted by two plain-clothes policemen, who demanded to see our passports. We realised that we had left them at the hotel and told them so. Rather than the four of us have to troop all of the way to the hotel, I asked if I might take them to a resident who would vouch for us. The older of the two, very stern-looking and with a severe moustache, appeared unwilling, but his young companion took pity on us and won him over. I took them to a nearby café that we had visited often when the family were over. I asked the proprietress, in front of the policemen, if she remembered us.

'Immediately you sat down!' she declared. 'And how are your daughters? Oh yes, I know you very well.'

That settled the matter, but we had to agree to go immediately to the hotel to collect our passports and keep them with us from that moment on.

We were concerned at this turn of events, which suggested a growing paranoia on behalf of the authorities. It was only this evening, when we heard the news on the wireless, that we fully appreciated that they had good reason, for although the evacuation of Dunkirk is complete, many French soldiers left behind have been captured, and the French 6th Army has been pushed back by the German 9th Army to the north of Soissons.

Friday 7th June

This morning Will complained of having perhaps suffered from the night air after dinner, as his arms and particularly his chest were more painful. He decided to stay the morning in bed.

I advised no lunch, it being a meatless day – so no ham, pork or by-products – and that I would arrange for a boiled egg at the café. He enjoyed it and seemed better, but the heat of a brooding storm was oppressive, and we sat quietly for an hour in the garden. Afterwards he took a walk, whilst I took tea, arranging to meet back at the apartment at 5pm.

After buying strawberries and other things, I began preparing a meal with these for Will, who I expected each minute to arrive with the car, bringing our things from the garage, because the charwoman and her husband were coming to help us unload them at 5.30pm. The heat was unbearable and so I lay on the chaise longue.

Will came in to say that he would start to unload and urged me to do the same, but I refused, saying that two hefty people would be here in a few minutes and I had been waiting to welcome him with a nice meal I had prepared.

He thoroughly enjoyed the meal, and afterwards saw to bringing up our store of petrol until we could hide it next day. Afterwards, we spent an hour talking in the garden, and on entering the house agreed that we had fallen on our feet here and were both very contented. Will would not eat supper but mixed us both some toddy, and we sat on my bed chatting. He felt that it would be wise for us to stay here for the duration, and that I should get used to the heat as he did in Australia years ago, and that we should make a start collecting pine cones and wood for next winter.

The fire grate looks useful. Will has given me a lot of matches and some candles, saying that on the first night in a strange house, it might be difficult to find the switches. Now he has gone to his room, but has just called out to tell me how fortunate he is to have two large windows on each side of the room.

Saturday 8th June

I can barely comprehend what has happened today.

This morning I went to Will's room as usual to ask how he had slept. I went to open the large French window and shook it, saying it was hard to open, and that we had no small trays for breakfast. Will is often quiet and sleepy in the morning and so I took no notice when he did not respond.

On drawing near to the bed, I looked hard at him as he was lying so still and appeared not to be breathing. I touched his arm. My last touch. I realised that he must have passed away a very short time before. I was choked by a terrible feeling of shock. I must have stood quite still for I do not know how long. Minutes at least. Looking and waiting. Expecting to see, as I have many times before, the slightest movement of his head. He was so often like this in the mornings, and I was convinced that he would suddenly awake. The awful stillness grew and grew, until it all but enveloped me. I could not, dared not, move. My feet were glued to the floor.

Eventually I became aware of the sound of a clock ticking somewhere in the apartment, and the voices of soldiers in the square outside. I sat on the bed, put my arms around my beloved Will, and kissed him on his cheek.

I tore myself away and went to find our landlady to ask her to send for the nearest doctor. Dr Feeze was out, and it was a long hour and a half before a different doctor came.

He was younger than Dr Feeze. Grave in demeanour but very kind. He examined Will and asked some questions as to his age and medical conditions. Then he surprised me by saying, 'I noticed a smell of gasoline as soon as I entered the apartment?'

I explained how Will had siphoned petrol into twelve cans so that we would have sufficient to enable us to return to England. That we had it unloaded yesterday with the intention of finding somewhere to store it until it was needed.

He nodded his head. 'It is as I thought,' he said. His expression softened, and a look of sadness passed over his face. 'I am sorry to tell you, Madame,' he continued, 'that your husband has died of gasoline inhalation. It is not uncommon, I am afraid, and you must remove these cans from your apartment as soon as possible.'

My legs threatened to give way. The doctor took my arm and led me to the wicker chair by the window. I had assumed that the rheumatic fever had finally caught up with Will – either that, or the heat. To discover that it was that damned petrol, and entirely avoidable, was too much to bear.

When the doctor left, I asked the landlady to tell me of someone who might prepare Will and tidy the room. She wanted to send for the charwoman, but I said no, and pleaded with her try to find someone more practised and professional. She spoke with another lady in the house, who suggested that I send for the Sisters of Mercy, which I did.

Despite the fact that neither Will nor I are of the faith, two of the Sisters came immediately. They told me that I should go at once to the Mairie to register Will's death, and to make arrangements for his interment, and leave the rest to them.

The landlady came with me to the Mairie. It was now 10.05am, which was problematic as between 10am and 12 noon, the officials are all busy giving out petrol. Each time the landlady approached the secretary, she was told that as our business was of longer duration, we must wait. The irony was not lost on me.

It was gone 11am by the time a grave was bought, and an Arab appointed as the gravedigger. I was told that it was not possible for Will to be laid to rest in the cemetery at St Paul as I wished. Instead, it would have to be in the little cemetery at Beauvallon. The time was fixed for 9am on Tuesday.

I was directed to a nearby joiner's shop where I might order a coffin. I was insistent upon an oak coffin, but he explained that in present circumstances, with so many men called up to the military, it was impossible to find enough oak and he could only offer to supply pitch pine. There was no brass on the coffin, and he explained that the trimmings and flowers could only be obtained by order, that it was now too late in the day, and the use of a telephone was forbidden.

It was now 11.45am and I was at last free to send a wire to Bill, informing him of his father's death. I hurried to the Bureau de Poste, where a Czech lady copied my writing into block letters in French, whilst I wrote about a dozen lines to go by airmail. I then had to go post-haste with the wire to get it stamped at the Mairie, as no telegram is accepted after 12 noon. I almost ran in the great heat and was just in time for the midday collection and the closing of the post office.

Whilst at the Mairie I had asked if Mr Birman, our neighbour from back home, whom I knew had been staying in St Pierre, was still alive as he had been seriously ill when we passed through in the autumn. The Secretary thought he had seen him some months ago.

When I reached home, Mr Birman followed me through the gate! Someone had heard me ask for him and told him so.

He came in, offering his condolences. He thoughtfully had brought a lunch of bread and cheese, which he spread on the table. It was the first food I had had since the strawberries and cream of yesterday. We sat in the garden and drank the wine left over from Will's and my picnic, which now seems like a hundred years ago. We reminisced for a while and then he reminded me of a conversation with Will a long time ago, when his mother's finger had tapped on the office window at Low

Fell. I remembered the incident and told him so.

We smiled at the memory of those happy times, and then he asked if he could see Will. I was glad that he wished to do so.

When he returned, he said, 'He looks so peaceful, and has regained much of his youthful appearance.'

I will treasure that comforting remark until the day I die. Mr Birman stayed for another hour or so. As he was leaving, the Sisters of Mercy came to complete their preparations. I gave them 100 francs for the church. I never saw Will again.

I went to queue again at the Mairie to finish my arrangements for the interment. The graves were in rows and numbered, and the prices varied according to their situation. I chose a site and was then asked which class of coach I would like. The first class has two horses with black and silver loincloths and bonnets with silver eyeholes, and large black fir trees or plumes on a very, very elaborately carved black coach. The assistants wear frock coats and silk hats. I have chosen the 2nd class and have decided to follow the coach in our car. This coach has a bay horse and white feet, and a very homely coach far more suited to my feelings.

Coming home, I found that I was physically and emotionally exhausted, and had no power to think. The landlady had closed the shutters, presumably because there had been a death in the house, and it was dark and cool in my bedroom. I lay down on my bed and stared at the ceiling.

Towards sunset, I made a cup of tea and then walked alone up the hill to the '*Panorama unique*', to see the sun set in the west, and its reflection on the snow behind St Paul in the east.

When I re-entered the apartment, I was struck by the overpowering smell of petrol. Remembering the doctor's warning, I carried the cans one by one into the kitchen. It was now 2am. I made some more tea and began this entry in my diary. Now that it is finished, I will take to bed one of my Italian novels – a romance, I think – in the hope that it will grip my attention until, God willing, I fall asleep.

Tuesday 11th June

I was up early this morning. The luggage had been put in both of our rooms but now it was all in mine, and I had difficulty finding black stockings and gloves because I had no idea which suitcase I had put them in. It ended up with our belongings strewn all over the place, and I had still not found them.

To make matters worse, I was now unable to find my bag containing all of our money and the car keys. I desperately needed the keys because my black shoes were in the back of the car.

I became desperately muddled. Under the one weak electric light, all of the belongings appeared as a single dead colour. I tried opening the shutters but the sun was too bright. I sat on the bed and sobbed. At last I pulled myself together, and slipped on the black costume I had only recently had made, never thinking that I should be wearing it for such an occasion.

Then I hurried down to the garage to hire a large car to take Mr Birman, myself, and two kind women, each bringing large bouquets of flowers from their own gardens. The landlady had made up a sheath of pink roses from a bush that Will had so recently admired. One of the women lent me some black shoes, and I resolved that I would have to do as I was. And thus we set off.

The Mayor had kindly sent word to the military barricade to allow us to pass without stamping our identity cards. After about two miles, we turned into the hills, and the route wound around many tight hairpin bends to the cemetery. It was a unique level spot with a marvellous view, quiet but not isolated, overlooking the town and gulf of St Tropez and, not too far away, the pre-Saracen town of Sainte Maxime.

I knew that neither industry nor noise would ever desecrate this hallowed place, and I felt relieved to be leaving Will there. On reflection, I realised that had we set off sooner, and had Will passed away on the journey, it might have been so different.

I cannot believe that today was Will's birthday, and that we did not get to celebrate it together. But I will always be thankful for, and take comfort from, our last picnic in the valley of the Plan de la Tour.

Mr Birman gave a very touching address, saying that although Will was being interred in a strange land, it was in a place that he loved. He had borrowed an English Bible from Commander Boyes of Grimaud, and read Jonas II, the words so fitting to our troubled days:

> 'For thou hadst cast me into the deep, in the midst of the seas; and the floods compassed me about: all thy billows and thy waves passed over me...the weeds wrapped about my head...afterwards the promise of resurrection.'

We were a mixed audience: Protestant, Quaker, Lutheran, Catholic and Arab. The men who carried the simple coffin were Mohammedans, and Mr Birman spoke to them and thanked them on my behalf. When we left, I promised myself that I would return there very soon.

Mr Birman came back with me to share his lunch and I shared mine with him. He had brought with him kind messages from friends and acquaintances of ours in St Pierre. His bright and interesting conversation was really helpful to me and passed the day, which would otherwise have been so desolate.

Wednesday 12th June

This morning I went into town to find someone to paint a Union Jack flag on a stone for Will's grave, because I could not bear the thought of it so plain and lonely, among all of the finer graves with their marble headstones and bowls of flowers. Unfortunately, the man to whom I was directed was not there. I will return tomorrow.

Later on, I went to the bazaar where Will had bought the pair of deckchairs to explain to the proprietor what has happened, and to ask if he might be able to resell them. He was most sympathetic and insisted on repayment in full.

I was back home in the act of making tea when I heard someone trying to open the garden gate. I went to look and found it was two English ladies. I told them to push hard on the gate, and come in.

They came in and asked if I were Mrs Powell and offered help if there anything that was in their power to assist me. I took them to my room, for the state of which I had to apologise as the chairs were overflowing with everything that I had removed from our cases in my haste to find my shoes and gloves and car keys for the funeral, and had not yet had the strength or inclination to repack. I piled everything on the bed, and we all sat down.

They introduced themselves as Miss Shipley and Miss Reynolds. They were both Quakers, like Will and me. Miss Shipley struck me as a very 'busy' person, brisk in manner and extremely able. She told me that she had spent her youth working in Newcastle for the 'British Women's Temperance Association', and it transpired that we had many friends and places in common. The other lady was a Miss Reynolds, sister to Edward Bassett Reynolds, the former sub-editor of the Quaker newspaper, *The Friend*. She was much quieter than her companion, and demure, but most sympathetic and eager to help.

I discovered that they have been three months in Chez Moi, the little house taken by Bill and Lorna for their honeymoon three years ago, and have only just moved into a villa close by. Before they left, they asked me to join them for tea tomorrow. I thanked them and asked if they would do me a great favour and drive me to Grimaud to find Miss McGregor, who I fancy might like to accompany me to England in the car and share the driving. They were only too happy to be able to help, and readily agreed to call for me at 9am tomorrow morning.

Thursday 13th June

We inquired at the first hotel for a very tall Scotch lady, a Miss McGregor, and were immediately told that she had left the day before to go to Pardigon, six miles away. Miss Shipley and Miss Reynolds insisted that they would take me there.

When we arrived at this second hotel, we were informed that she was out, and would probably be found on the shore, half a mile away.

I left the ladies at the hotel and walked down to sea, hoping that this was not a fool's errand. But there she was, under an erection covered with palm leaves, looking for all the world like a South Sea Island Queen.

She was very pleased to see me, although much saddened to hear of Will's passing. Once we had got past her condolences, I explained my proposition, and she readily agreed. I left the book of car papers, as she now proposes to go to Nice on Tuesday to see the Consul and the AA Association as she needed a licence, which she does not currently hold, and also to get her exit visa.

I told her that I would accompany her as I also need an exit visa and, with so many military on the move, I believe it wise to ask the AA to advise me on the best route to England.

By now the temperature was in the mid-seventies and I was covered in perspiration by the time I had climbed back up to the hotel.

Miss Shipley and Miss Reynolds drove me to the furnished villa into which they were still settling. They brought out a simple but welcome tea and we sat chatting in the garden, they in the sun, and me in the shade. It transpires that they have lived together for 14 years. I was not in the least surprised as they are so relaxed together, and such excellent company. I enjoyed my afternoon as much as circumstances allowed, since all things now are comparative. But, from out of the blackness has come this ray of light, and their kindness is amplified tenfold.

I asked them to set me down a little way from the apartment, as the temperature had dropped and there was a cooling breeze from off the hills. As I was nearing home, I saw a little dog – a white poodle – that appeared familiar, and sure enough into view came its owner, Mrs Palmer, a French lady who was born in America and who lives with her American husband in a villa a little higher up the hill. She recognised me at once and insisted that I join her for an early supper this evening and stay to hear the news. I readily agreed. Anything is preferable to being alone.

When I arrived at the villa, Mr Palmer was working in the garden accompanied by a local gardener. He explained that he had been meaning to rearrange the garden ever since he had bought this place several years ago, and he was now making some sort of rockery, and choosing which plants to purchase.

Mr Palmer is typically American: very confident, talkative and direct. His wife's Frenchness shines through, notwithstanding the time she has spent in America. She is very gay and continually makes jokes against herself and the rest of the family that puts one at ease. They have one daughter, Louise – about 17, I think – educated in England. The three of them, feeling that Sainte Maxime was a safety zone, had come from their Paris flat much earlier in the season than usual. They are a lovely family and I like them very much.

Mrs Palmer and I discovered a mutual interest in the prophesies of Nostradamus, the special magician to Marie de Medici. We spent quite a while discussing the possible relevance of his prophecies to the warfare unfolding before us.

The Germans have just made the 'Bulge' but somehow this didn't disquiet us. Both Mr and Mrs Palmer had been writing to America. This had occupied the previous week and their letters seemed plaintive and yet forceful enough to be used as propaganda amongst their acquaintances regarding the French situation.

The Germans were making headway towards Paris. We again discussed Nostradamus, who prophesised the Germans reaching Lyon – what a ridiculous idea – utterly impossible – the Americans would never leave France in the lurch – something would be done! We learned from the newspapers and the wireless that the French line was unbroken, and everyone had faith in General Weygand. I could not help being hurt, however, by the constant assertion by the press that there were no British in France and the French were bearing all the brunt alone, having no reinforcements to relieve the poor tired men who had been fighting on the front for many days. 'Where are the British?' the Germans asked. 'At home!' they replied.

On the way home, I saw nine planes fly over at St Tropez, where there is a torpedo factory and a new electric power station. It is four days now since Mussolini declared war on France and Britain, so I was not surprised to see Italian markings on the planes.

They arranged themselves in formation like hawks, and let fall their shells or bombs, making little puffs of smoke against the sky. All of their bombs fell into the Mediterranean, and as they were leaving the anti-aircraft guns came into action, striking two of the planes. One fell like lead, directly into the sea. The other glided over the woods and disappeared. Then a huge cloud of black smoke rose above the trees. It was fortunate that the fire did not spread further as forest fires are much feared hereabouts, and volunteers are out night and day at this time with everything dry, and so much undergrowth covered with pine needles.

It was troubling that the district air raid warning had not worked. Children were playing in the streets, and no one had taken shelter.

Despite all of the bad news, and the portents heralded by the air raid, I entered my apartment feeling better for the warmth and genuineness of the Palmers' welcome, and their kind entertainment.

Friday 14th June

At midnight last night, I heard the thrum of one of the aeroplanes returning. I had not been to sleep and so I went out onto the terrace to see if I could catch sight of it. It appeared to drop its bomb over St Tropez. Judging by the sound and fury of the blast, it must have been unnerving in its perfection. The remainder of the night was very noisy from the crowded streets. The news that Italy gave out this morning was that St Tropez had gone up in flames, leaving the town in ashes. Damnable lie!

During the last few days, Sainte Maxime has become quite empty, much of the military having left, and only sailors on guard at the new bridge by the port.

This evening I went again to the Palmers' villa. The three of them had just returned from a visit to the American and Spanish Consuls in Marseilles. The two air raids yesterday had filled them with fear for Louise should the enemy come. They told me they intended go to Lisbon for America, but after their visit to the American Consul, an air raid warning had sent them scurrying into a shelter in a cul-de-sac and when the all-clear sounded, they found that the Spanish Consulate was closed.

From the wireless we learned that the Germans were approximately 50 miles, or 80km, from Paris. An awful depression filled the house. To make matters worse, an elderly couple who had fled from Brussels and were staying in a house nearby, arrived to introduce themselves and to share their story.

They had just started up their little car to begin the journey from Brussels when they heard the noise of the advancing German Army. Seeing a tank appearing at the bend in the road, they leaped from the car and ran into the fields to escape. Fortunately, they had a quantity of money and jewellery on them and were able to use this to make their way to Sainte Maxime.

When they left, Mrs Palmer was close to despair. I tried to comfort her, pointing out that they were Americans and need not fear. But their concern was for Louise, who must be got away at all costs. Mr Palmer, less inclined to panic, was advising patience. In the end, I realised that Mrs Palmer was right and urged her husband to hasten their arrangements to leave. He was, after all, much older than his wife, and at 74 years of age more vulnerable than I think he realised. I could not but think of Will, and how what had happened to him should not be repeated with them.

Saturday 15th June

Paris was entered yesterday by the Germans. Thank God that General Weygand had declared an open city and so the German Army was able to enter unopposed and without doing the kind of damage to the city prophesied by Nostradamus. We heard that the shops were open and that everything was business as usual. But this must have been exaggerated as we know that the French Government is now at Tours, and many of the head offices are as far away from Paris as Bordeaux.

My landlady goes to her friend each day to listen to the wireless, sometimes including German broadcasts. She comes back with such garbled stories that I have long ceased to believe her.

On the way to the bakery, I encountered the Czech lady of my acquaintance. She told me that her husband, who is an officer in the French army, has told her that they now have only a standing army of 35,000 regular men, plus the conscripts. He stated that there was no way that they could withstand the whole weight of the German Army, having lost so many of their own men when they were inveigled into Belgium by the English. I was at a loss to know how to respond, and merely expressed my sympathy, made my apologies, and left.

I met Mrs Palmer inside the bakery. She was in a state of high panic, but when I finally managed to calm her, she invited me to tea again. On leaving the bakery, I went to the market to buy fruit. Miss McGregor came towards me, waving frantically. She told me that she had posted a letter to me yesterday, urging me to put off leaving Sainte Maxime with her just yet, as the roads are full of refugees from Paris and the North, and she believes it would be quieter and safer to travel in a few days' time. We had intended going to St Malo where I thought we might get on one of the potato boats to St Helier in Jersey, because I was concerned that the escaping military might take up the ordinary traffic. I decided to agree to her request on the grounds that a few days' rest would be better on my nerves.

Miss McGregor and I took lunch together so that we might discuss the arrangements for our journey. We ended by agreeing that I should phone her at her hotel in Pardigon, should anything occur to cause us to change our plans.

After lunch I needed to go to the bank as I had not yet paid the municipal costs of Will's funeral. Imagine my concern when I discovered that the bank had stopped our account because of Will's death and would not release any money. I requested to speak to the manager, whom I pleaded to waive the rules as I was English and given the state of the country and the war, I must leave France as soon as possible. He flew into a rage, claiming that all of France's suffering had been caused by England, and that if I did not leave immediately, he would phone the police to have me put out!

The money that Will and I had arranged, we thought would have lasted us at least two years if we lived quietly. Now that I am alone, it will last even longer. But if the bank does not release it, I shall barely have enough to leave France, let alone to live on. I began to bristle at the perpetual grumbling here against England, particularly since I feel that it is now France that is making me suffer.

On reflection I cannot believe that the money is truly lost, and I shall go to the British Consulate in Nice on Monday to ask them to assist me in persuading the bank to release my funds.

When I arrived at the Palmers' villa, I was in low dudgeon, but I resolved to hide it from them. They have worries of their own. Mrs Palmer asked if I would help her to sew their beautiful Persian carpets into white linen sheets so that they would be safe on their journey to America. I was more than happy to oblige. Mr Palmer has collected many beautiful rugs and carpets for the walls and the beautiful oatmeal-tiled floors. Now I knew that they were really going!

Poor Mrs Palmer. I found her crying in the kitchen. When I asked her what the matter was, she said that she was crying for Paris. She quoted a line from today's newspaper:

'Paris had never been so dear to her children as now. There are no tourists, they have it to themselves, and the gardens never looked so exquisite as in this favourable spring. And now it is occupied by the hated Germans.'

When I arrived home, the landlady urged me to rest, as she could see that such disorder was clearly wearing for me. She said that the rooms were paid for until the month expired, and I should put my things in order, and then I should feel more settled. She clearly does not understand that I am unable to rest. I have given all my days to my husband. I miss supporting him. I miss his presence, and his voice. He talked and read aloud to me every day for the past forty-three years, and the absence of that is indescribable. I have no choice. I must either leave, or busy myself with something. My work has come to an end, and the uselessness of arranging my clothes, and tidying the apartment is a futile way to fill the time.

Sunday 16th June

I am relieved that I have decided to leave. Eighteen months ago, I was at a meeting where someone said that England would declare war on Germany. Nothing in the world seemed more improbable. Yet now I am just waiting for these things to unfold before me in cold blood.

I don't know what is happening to the French. They seem stunned. The day after the Italians declared war, there were no fresh vegetables or fruit in the market, and there was a feeling of deadness over the whole district. I forgot to say that just before we left St Paul, Mme and Mlle Serraire and their son came up in a taxi to take what rooms there were in the house. They were frightened to death. How strange it is that they have so little faith in their own people. I feel a great lack of unity right now towards France, when we used to be so close. I realise that they have their problems. Not just the invasion, but all of the refugees from across Europe and France heading south. And apparently no one here will buy War Bonds on which the Government depends, since gathering taxes in France is now nigh on impossible. How will it all end?

Mr Birman told me today that the Dublimans, who live near Chez Moi, having given two million francs to the war, he was given a colonelship in the army – but that here he is at home, not liking the army. He also told of another younger man in Sainte Maxime, who whilst at home on leave went to hospital for three weeks, and got himself invalided out. Such is the morale of their army now.

This morning I went again to queue at the Mairie to get permission to travel to St Malo, and before that to Nice so that I might see the Consul, to try to get my money released. I queued for one and a half hours. It seemed that everybody else was getting petrol coupons and so I took the opportunity to ask for one myself. I was given 10 gallons, which I am sure will come in handy on my journey.

When I finally reached the head of the queue, I was told that foreigners seeking a laissez-passer permit for Nice and St Malo must go to Draguignan, twenty-four miles away, to get one from the Prefect. I was so tired, I said never, and that if I must die here, then so be it. The Mayor suggested that I take a taxi, which was about 250 francs. I told him that because of the bank's failure to release my money, I could not afford it, nor could I risk using up my precious petrol. He immediately relented and gave me a pass as a resident of Sainte Maxime.

As I was leaving, someone told me that an English lady was waiting outside to see me. She asked if she could come with me to Pau if that was where I was going. I told her that I was going to St Malo. 'Oh, that awful place,' she said. 'No, no, I must go to Pau.' She then explained that she had planned to leave with two English people in her hotel but, saying nothing to her, they had left early this morning to board a warship at Cannes. She had tried to procure a taxi in order to follow them, but it had proved impossible.

I tried to comfort her by saying that she might have had a lucky escape as I had heard that Cannes had just been heavily bombed. I told her that it was my intention to go to Nice after lunch. She gave me a note to the Consul asking him to wire her what to do. I took it. It was the least I could do. People are increasingly in much distress.

After lunch, the landlady came back with the awful news that Pétain had asked for an armistice, and that France could not go on alone with their soldiers exhausted and too few men or materials. There were no English to help, she said. They ought never to have gone to Belgium and left France unguarded.

I could not believe that the French were about to surrender and felt that she must have heard it from the German news. I hurried up to the Palmers to see what they had heard. Louise was in on her own. She confirmed the news just as I had been told by my landlady and made almost exactly the same comment about poor France. Saying that now they had lost Paris, and England had abandoned her, what else could they possibly do but sue for peace?

I was speechless. What could I say? I just hung my head, said nothing, and left, intending to drive up later to say goodbye.

I sat on my bed with my head in my hands. There was an ache in the pit of my stomach, and I had a cold feeling of dread at this melting down of French resistance. The armistice was almost upon us. First Belgium, now the French, and little England left to stand alone against the German might. What would become of us?

Eventually I pulled myself together, and decided to phone Miss McGregor at the Pardigon Hotel to see if she had heard the news and, if so, what she made of it.

Immediately she answered the telephone, Miss McGregor said, 'Have you heard the news?' I replied, 'I have. What is the next step?' 'There are a number of us here at this hotel,' she said, 'and we are all going to a destroyer at Cannes this afternoon. Will you come? It is better to get away immediately as we are now in enemy country.'

I was stunned. Only three days before, she had asked me to stay until she got a visa and permit to drive to St Malo. But for that, I would by now be almost at St Malo. I told her that I was not ready. I had not finished packing. Besides, my intention was to get back to England with the car and all of my possessions.

I went home and immediately began to pack. There was so much stuff, far more than when I came. Will was marvellous at packing and had been so much cleverer than I in getting so much in such a small space, even with our twelve one-gallon tins of petrol. I have done my best, trying to recall how he had managed it, but there are still possessions I have no option but to leave behind. And I still could not access my money.

I had tea very early, and the Czech lady very kindly went with me to the house of the Deputy Mayor to entreat him on my behalf. She was well acquainted with him, and explained that he was a native of Strasbourg, and a harder man to deal with than the Provençals, but she would do her best. It was a long walk out into the countryside, and the sun was merciless for this time of year. The cigales[40] mocked us with their incessant, shrill 'reep-reep-reep-reep-reep' from the trees along the side of the road.

He greeted us courteously and listened intently as my Czech lady pleaded with him to use his influence with the bank manager to persuade him to release my money. I showed him the note that I had been given, requiring me to pay at the Mairie what was owing on Will's funeral. He promised that he would do what he could in the morning and suggested that I go to the Mairie at around 11am. That made the long walk back feel much less onerous, helped by the setting of the sun and the cooling breeze.

Today has been physically and emotionally exhausting. I believe I shall have no difficulty sleeping tonight.

---

[40] The symbol of Provence, known in English as the cicada. According to Provençal folklore, God sent these noisy insects to disturb the peasants' siestas so they would be forced to return to their work.

Monday 17th June

Disappointment awaited me at the Mairie. I was standing in the queue when the Deputy Mayor arrived and came to speak with me.

He explained that he had indeed gone to the bank first thing to plead on my behalf, but the wretched bank manager claimed that as he had to wait for authorisation from his headquarters and was still awaiting a response, there was no possibility of his releasing the money today. My heart sank, and I was about to leave when the Mayor's secretary came to me, saying that she had overheard our conversation and I was not to concern myself. The situation had already been explained to the Mayor, and he had decided that I could leave Sainte Maxime without settling the bill! This act of kindness has restored my faith in the French.

My appetite was restored; I had an omelette of two eggs for lunch. Then I set about preparing some emergency rations for my journey, lest there be shortages along the way. I stewed a bone to make stock for a soup and boiled a few eggs hard. I added two tins of sardines and some tinned milk to my pack, and finally decided that I was ready to leave. I will keep my diary with the papers for the car as I intend to carry on these entries when I can, both as a distraction and a record.

As was saying my goodbyes to the landlady, the Catholic priest arrived. He had heard that I was planning to leave, and wanted to reassure me, saying that the armistice idea was just a rumour put out by the Germans, and in fact a wilful lie. I thanked him for his concern, but it has not weakened my resolve. There is no reason for me to stay, and every reason to go.

Tuesday 18th June

I left the apartment at six this evening, driving back towards La Nartelle to say goodbye to my two Quaker friends, Miss Shipley and Miss Reynolds, who had been so supportive, and whom I could not leave without thanking. They were insistent that I change my route and head to Bordeaux, as the Germans have taken Cherbourg. They wrote down a route and marked it on the map we keep in the car. They also gave me some addresses to write to on my arrival in England, both to assure their friends of their safety, and in case I should need any assistance.

It was after 7pm that I started on my long lonely journey, and Sainte Maxime seemed deserted as I left. It was my intention to drive for four to five hours and get as close to Bordeaux as possible. Over the past week or so, the nights have been as clear as day, and tonight was also clear but with some heavy thunder to the north, behind the mountains.

As I turned west, I made good time until the sky began to darken, the rumble of thunder drew ever closer, and I found that I was running into a storm. Towards Grimaud the rain became intense, drumming on the bonnet of my car and on the hard warm ground like bullets from a thousand guns. A dense white mist rose up in front of me. With the roof closed, I was unable to see over the windscreen and so I had to take refuge in a sawmill at the side of the road.

When a break appeared in the storm, I set off again. Ahead I caught glimpses every now then of the ruined chateau of Grimaud on the hills above, rising out of the mist, and was reassured that I was heading in the right direction.

At this point, the screen-wiper was struggling to do its work, and even with the top now open, it was difficult to see clearly. In consequence, I could only travel at twelve miles an hour. Despite the fact that I was soaking wet and cold, I felt relieved to be on the road. But oh, how many barricades there were across the road! Each time one appeared through the gloom, I was forced to change down through the gears with a crunch and a grind, and an arm-wrenching twist, when Will had made it look so easy!

Every three miles or so, soldiers emerged from the gloom carrying lanterns, and forced me to stop and show my note of *laissez-passer*, and *carte d'identité*. In every case they began by demanding to know if I was Italian. Heaven knows what they plan to do with those they catch.

Throughout this stretch of my journey along the route nationale through Aix-en-Provence, I felt so very far from home, and from my family and friends, and overcome by a sense of total isolation. Although the rain had stopped, clouds obscured the moon, and it was much darker than normal. Here was I, still travelling at twelve miles an hour, when the German Army, aided by clear skies, has made such unparalleled progress – fifty miles, day and night, with their infantry and reconnaissance.

The part of my journey to Le Luc led me along hairpin bends that cut through woods and ran along deep gorges. I recalled their exceptional beauty in daylight, but even now there was special majesty about them, accompanied by the sharp, sweet scent of pine. I suppose that had it been daylight, I might have seen the slashes in the bark where the resin is draining down into the cups waiting to receive it.

The further I went, the more anxious I was to get on. Imagine my relief when I arrived at route N7, and found the barricades deserted, and not a soldier in sight. And later, when I saw the only living being I had seen – a woman – since I left Sainte Maxime, which had been deserted. I didn't doubt that they were there somewhere, alert to any possible incursion of the Italian Army. But for the moment, all seemed silent and eerie in the early morning mist.

I saw a woman standing by the door of her cottage and pulled up. I asked her if war had ceased on account of the promised armistice? She shrugged, and said, 'I do not know, but I hope so.' I told her that I had not seen any soldiers along the grande route, and asked if she knew where they had gone? 'They have gone to rest,' she said, 'having been on guard all night as it was late.'

Towards midnight, I came to Aix-en-Provence and decided to stop. I calculated that I had travelled seventy-two miles but was still forty-eight miles short of my original objective, which was Arles. I was wet and cold and exhausted, and had no option but to go in search of a room for the night. I followed a cloudburst into the city. The streets were running rivers of water, just as they had been when we stayed here for three days last year while Will recovered from a severe attack of rheumatism. Of all of the other cars on the route, mine was the only one to head into the centre ville. My headlights shone on the wet streets like mirrors.

I found a number of hotels open, but none had beds available. I had been warned way back in St Paul that there was not a bed to be had in the whole of France, and so it proved. In one hotel, the manager even phoned through to contacts he had in Pau to see if they might have a room for me, but without success. He explained to me that on the radio, the public had been told not to move from where they were, and that the movement of supplies of food had ceased.

A youth saw me standing by the car after my futile efforts to find a bed and came asking if he could help. I said that I wanted something to eat, but all of the cafés and restaurants were closed. He told me that he had a friend who owned a little restaurant and although now closed – on account of Pétain's last, mad directive that all eateries must close at 10pm – I could go in and eat by knocking at the back door. He offered to take me there.

Sure enough, his friend, the proprietor, ushered me in, and served me a simple meal of a few tinned peas, bread and beer, which I enjoyed as though it were a feast! But my tired nerves were irritated by the uproarious sound of a fountain outside that had far too much water to play with after the rain. The waitress was still busy washing up and tidying around, and the proprietor told me that I could stay until she went home about 2am.

When I had finished eating, the proprietor joined me for polite conversation. I heard a heavy rumble of traffic on the road nearby, and feared they might be the German or Italian troops. I asked him the cause of so much noise – was the military moving? He replied that it was the refugees from the North and had been continuous for the past four days. Having had no news since yesterday noon, I asked him where exactly the German positions in the North were, as it was my intention to go to Bordeaux to find a ship for England? He said that I should leave as soon as possible as the Germans would very soon reach Nantes, less than one hundred and eighty miles from Bordeaux.

I immediately decided to change my plans. I was determined to embark for England with both my car and all of my possessions. With the Germans so close to Bordeaux, I could not risk going there and decided to head instead for Lisbon. I left at 2am, in the dark and mist, fed and dry, but more anxious than ever.

Wednesday 19th June

I reached Arles at 6am. None of the cafés were open for breakfast but I found a workers' place near the station, where people coming off duty were having rum and other stimulants.

I ordered some very good strong coffee with milk and some bread. The proprietor apologised that the bread was stale, but I persevered and used it to dip in my coffee. Not being French, I normally abominate coffee used as soup, but after two of these coffees, I felt like another person, and settled back to read yesterday's paper. In the paper was printed the text of a speech by Mr Churchill to Parliament yesterday. I have it here and have copied it as best I can.

*'What General Weygand called the Battle of France
is over. I expect that the Battle of Britain is about to
begin. Upon this battle depends the survival of
Christian civilisation. Upon it depends our own
British life, and the long continuity of our institutions
and our Empire. The whole fury and might of the
enemy must very soon be turned on us.*

*Hitler knows that he will have to break us in
this Island or lose the war. If we can stand up to him,
all Europe may be free, and the life of the world may
move forward into broad, sunlit uplands. But if we
fail, then the whole world, including the United
States, including all that we have known and cared
for, will sink into the abyss of a new Dark Age made
more sinister, and perhaps more protracted, by the
lights of perverted science.*

*Let us therefore brace ourselves to our duties,
and so bear ourselves, that if the British Empire and
its Commonwealth last for a thousand years, men
will still say, 'This was their finest hour.'*

I found this somehow both chilling and inspirational.
Either way, I strengthened my resolve to conclude my
journey, and return home to England.

An hour had passed, and I felt truly rested for the
first time since leaving Sainte Maxime. Then the sky
turned black, and I hurried to my car, feeling like one
might when trying to escape from the Last Judgement.

I was now able to drive at fifty to sixty miles an hour,
and there were far fewer barricades. Each of these,
however, was very well guarded and overseen by
officers. The first few of these barricades were manned
by ordinary Senegalese, who were very conscientious but
not quite as efficient as the French.

The story was very different when I reached the
outskirts of Montpellier. Here was a whole army of
interrogators, who seemed to block the way for the
falling world to enter the safety zone. They forbade my

entry into this haven, claiming that it required a special visa issued that day from the Prefect at Nîmes. Hoping that he would not check the cans, I argued that I had no petrol, the gauge being quite empty. The officer assured me that there was a pump in a nearby town and pointed out a tiny Saracen fortress resembling St Paul, clinging to the top of a steep-sided hill.

I made my tour on a twisty road to the turn indicated to buy petrol and, on arriving, walked the narrow streets trying to find the filling station. I even thought that I might be safe in such a place as soon we should have thousands of planes to stop the unearthly progress of the Germans and a scheduled arrival in captured territory. All the population here were women and children, I never saw a man, and I was told that even the cellars and outhouses were taken by evacuees from Paris and the North. Eventually I found the filling station, which was inside a shop, a wretched and dilapidated property.

When I said that I sought to buy petrol, the girl in charge of the pump told me that there was no more to buy. I tried to persuade her, saying I was going to Bordeaux to catch an English boat. When she still refused, I said that perhaps if I were to give someone a tip, I might find some later? Her manner changed, and she said, 'Oh, I will give you some,' and magicked a gallon can from under a sack!

By now, the heavens had opened, and the rain cascaded from the rooftops, flooding the drains and transforming the narrow streets into rivers. The inside of the car was filling with water, and I sat there like a drowned rat. The girl called a friend to help and the three of us managed to close the roof.

Her friend was just arrived from Marseilles, which had been heavily bombed and everyone evacuated. When I told him that I was making for Nîmes to get a pass to enter Montpellier, he said, 'If you are, you will be cut off, as the Germans are at Nîmes.'

On asking an officer on the road out if the Germans were truly in Nîmes, he replied, 'No, they are not, but they were in Vienne last night. You must be careful because as you are English, you will be detained.'

Suddenly the roads were clogged with all these evacuees, with their beds and belongings on trailers and on the tops of cars, fleeing for their lives. It seemed to me that they might just as easily have stayed at home, as there was no petrol and no food.

Five miles from Nîmes, I stopped at a red light crossing, and a French soldier approached. He told me he was a ship's engineer and had often been to London, and hoped I might give him a lift to Nîmes? By now the rain had ceased, and I had managed to lower the roof to dry the interior of the car. Although there was no room for him to sit, he was able to arc himself over the luggage, and we proceeded thus.

I asked him why there were so many groups of soldiers and tanks standing still on the roads? There must have been thousands of them. I wondered if they were going to England, because I had been told that the French Navy was in Alexandria and Algeria, and their Air Force in Britain, so perhaps an effort would be made to get these trained men away from France. He said he had no idea, having had no news. I then remembered that I had never seen any of the soldiers with newspapers, and I assumed that they were even more in the dark than me.

When we arrived at the outskirts of the city, I was forced to park the car and proceed on foot. I asked if the naval officer would take me to the Prefect's office to get a pass to Montpellier and the Spanish frontier, en route to Portugal. The staff at the Mairie were unable to help, but sent a gendarme with me to the office of an agent de voyage, the head of which was most helpful and said I could have a pass to any place I wished at once. This was such a surprise that I was unable to decide on the spot. I know that I was vacillating and can only explain it by my lack of food and mental exhaustion.

He said, 'You must tell me now. It is time to close the office until 2 o'clock.' I said that I would like to consult my map and take a coffee to clear my head before deciding. I had only just made the momentous decision to go to Portugal instead of Bordeaux, and I was not sure of the route. I needed to think out the best way. I knew that Perpignan was somewhere to the south-east, but I had no idea of the distance, or if this was the most direct route. I promised to return at 2pm and went in search of a café.

I took coffee in a crowded café, the atmosphere electric with anxiety and a cacophony of sundry foreign languages. The wireless was on full blast, giving out the news in French, which in itself was not conducive to clear decision-making. What was evident from the map was that Bordeaux was more than four times the distance to Perpignan and the border at Figueres. And then I could see no clear route across the mountains to Lisbon, over eight hundred miles away, where Will and I have friends – the Watsons, who own watering stations for ships. I folded up my map and went back to the car, which I had left close to the arena. I sat there in silence, savouring peace, trying to get my head around the problem.

There came a tap at the window. When I looked up, I saw a young man standing there, accompanied by a young woman. They both appeared extremely nervous. I lowered the window, and he asked me if I happened to be going to Bordeaux. I told him that I was going to Lisbon as I had friends there, and asked if he was English since, although his accent was perfect, he did not look it.

He explained that he was a law student waiting to be called to the Bar. He and his wife had been on honeymoon in the Alps when the war broke out. They needed urgently to return to England where he was to sign on for a commission. His wife, he said, was much upset, as was he, having come from the Alps to Lyon en route for St Malo. After several days attempting to get a train, when they finally got there, they found the city surrounded by Germans, so took their rucksacks and left in haste. The French police told them that it was impossible for them to find means of transit as all roads were blocked, and the railway stations in German hands. However, they heard of a goods train which was taking refugees and managed to squeeze into an already overcrowded horsebox. Early the next morning, they arrived here in Nîmes.

They had bought two of the best bicycles procurable, intending to head for Bordeaux, which they hoped to reach in five days.

The journey in the horsebox, he said, had been a nightmare. There was the heat and smell of the horses, and of unwashed human bodies – the poor soldiers, who had slept where they stood from weariness. The discomfort and the incessant quarrelling was indescribable. He said he would give anything if I could give them and their cycles a ride to Bordeaux. He had a set of real pearl studs and his wife had her pearls, but they had very little money.

I told him that I must first go to the office to get my travel permit for the road and he said he could take me to the place where they had got their stamps to go by cycle. That turned out to be the Mairie, and I made my way there on my own. The officer had not come back from lunch. After having waited so long that I became uneasy, I decided to find the bureau where I had been earlier this morning, it now having passed 2pm. I got lost in the crowded streets and no one I stopped had heard of the place, not even the policemen.

Everywhere I went I received contradictory advice. One policeman told me I should go back to Sainte Maxime as Nîmes was a ringed military centre! Another told me I must come again tomorrow, and then I could have my visa and pass.

I went back to the car and found the two English people still waiting; I had forgotten all about them. Mr Reid, for that was his name, promised that if I took them, and in consequence lost my car and belongings, he would compensate me with a replacement car and the other costs. He also offered to share or take on the driving, saying he was a member of the Automobile Club and an excellent driver. By now I was too weary to argue, and so agreed. They immediately took me back to the Mairie. The officer was now in, but I was told that I must wait my turn. Finally, at 6.30pm, I had my pass for Bordeaux. We returned to my car, where Mr Reid wrote out the agreement on the back of an old insurance letter.

While he did so, I sat there still in two minds, feeling that Lisbon was a better option, with the Watsons, who had visited our home in Wigton Hall, and would be better placed to help me. But I was exhausted, and I knew that it would have been a long and uncertain journey for me on my own.

I have copied the agreement below, in case the original should become mislaid:

> *'19th June 1940*
> *I, Walter Joseph Reid, hereby declare that in consideration that Mrs Kate Powell takes me and my wife to catch the boat being provided for British refugees at Bordeaux, I shall be responsible for the loss of her car, and any of her clothes and possessions if, by reason of going to Bordeaux and not to the Spanish frontier in the Eastern Pyrenees, she should lose the same.*
> *The car I shall replace by a new one of the latest model, and the same horse power and type.*
> *I now assume all responsibility.*
> *The Royal Automobile Club, Pall Mall, London.'*

Reid and I both signed the agreement, and had it stamped by a local notary. I placed it in a cardboard envelope and put it in the glovebox with the other papers for the car.

I know that by taking them, I am sure to lose my car and most of my possessions, but I am beginning to think it may still be the best option. What if I were to have an accident in the Spanish mountains, or if Spain were to go over to the Germans? Besides, I cannot help thinking that this could easily have been Bill and Lorna on their honeymoon, and I would wish someone to take pity on them. I knew the Reids would have difficulty finding someone else to take them, and here am I with, thanks to Will, everything needed for the exodus – even a flashlamp, a towing rope, and a fresh tin of oil. Not to mention 18 gallons of petrol, including the tankful and the cans, when there is none to be had elsewhere.

In order to accommodate the Reids and their bikes, I had to divest myself of most of my possessions. I asked directions to the Salvation Army, where I asked for a Red Cross depot, where I then deposited three boxes of goods: all Will's good new suits as well as a brand-new dressing gown, eighteen pairs of socks, and three new sets of woven Wolsey underwear. In all, about £60 pounds' worth of goods, together with stuff of mine, and the value of the trunks.

Reid was anxious to start, but I was busy searching for Will's red silk handkerchief as a souvenir. The girls had bought it for him in Cambridge, together with a tie, as a gift. Reid became increasingly impatient and said they would go on alone if I did not take them. I knew it was a bluff.

At last we were ready. We sat in the Salvation Army yard planning the route. It was one that Dorothy and I had travelled in the autumn of 1936: Montpellier, Béziers, Narbonne and Toulouse, which I had always wished to visit and from where the grey geese come that we eat every Christmas. I told them that route included a very wet district. Mr Reid said if the car failed, he and his wife would go on alone on their bikes, but that I should not worry as he was an excellent chauffeur.

Before we set off, Mrs Reid and I shared the hard-boiled eggs I had brought from Sainte Maxime and also drank from a bottle the stewed bone water – a little high now with fermentation. Mr Reid took bread and butter and some tinned sardines and a glass of wine. At midnight, thus fortified, and with no need to stop en route except to keep up our supply of petrol, we set off, hoping to make good time before the roads became congested.

Thursday 20th June

By 2pm, despite our good intentions, we all became quite tired and Reid stopped at a touring place called Sartis, where we had some luck as we were given permission to sleep on the café benches for two hours. The Reids slept – Mr Reid had Will's warm overcoat on as well as his own to cover himself – but I was too cold, and only slept in fits and starts.

I was awoken by the feeling that someone was trying to start the car, so I woke Reid, who was as dead as a sack of corn. I shook him unmercifully for though the car was safe, the road was now full of refugees on foot as well as overloaded vehicles.

Barricades appeared at increasingly frequent intervals, and although at times we made more than 60mph we did not make the desired progress. We passed Carcassonne in the early morning, but the fog was such that we were denied the glorious pinnacles and turrets that make it the magical fairy castle that Dorothy and I had seen in a golden dawn four years ago.

Our next objective was Toulouse, a very fine and modern city much like Montpellier, through which we tore at breakneck speed. Such has been the weather today that England seemed by comparison a dry and arid country, and the English fogs, so often derided, a calumny on our mild and perfect climate.

We arrived at Bordeaux around 2pm, having driven approximately 800km as a result of numerous diversions.

Almost delirious with relief at having reached our destination, we headed straight for the British Consulate.

The street was lined with people, and the road full of parked vehicles. Reid asked a French officer to point out the Consulate. Imagine our dismay when he replied that it had closed, and the Consul had already gone to London. However, he said, a Pro-Consul would be found at Bayonne, a distance of 175km. No wonder then that there were so many crestfallen faces gazing at the empty building ahead of us. The officer also told us that the harbour had been heavily bombed the night before, and much damage had been done. One of the refugee boats leaving earlier from the port had been sunk, but all aboard had been saved. In consequence, he said, the refugee boats for England were now leaving from Bayonne.

We wheeled around at once, and without looking further, took the road to Bayonne, hoping to get there before the bureau closed. Reid sped through this beautiful city, past the beautiful parks, and the impressive grey stone monuments and public buildings. I pleaded with them to stop so that I could at least have a cup of tea.

On the outskirts of the city, we came across a tea garden where the proprietor had made a great effort at catering. Mrs Reid and I had tea with milk and two petite croissants about two inches long. Mr Reid pulled out his German sausage, which he had bought before having left Switzerland, now quite high after its sojourn in Lyon and in the horsebox en route to Nîmes. In the terrible heat of the thundery weather, we refused his offer to share it! Twenty minutes later, we were on our way again, on this most hectic and dangerous journey of my life.

We were not alone in racing to Bayonne. The road was like the entrance from a fowl house when the slide is lifted from the little outlet and all the fowl try to crash through at the same time. Many of the cars were as big as pantechnicons, powerful and speedy, with little care for the weaker. Everyone, it seemed, was all intent on leaving France either by boat or by crossing into Spain.

Mr Reid was by now exceptionally worked up and was convinced that he and his wife must be prepared to escape on their bicycles as both of them were sure to be shot if caught by the Germans! He seems to give no thought to what might happen to me. Perhaps he thinks because I am not of military age, they would not regard me as a threat? If so, I pray he is right.

At every checkpoint we are questioned thoroughly, as most of his and his wife's passport stamps are in German. He is very nervous on being asked why he is touring France. He tells them he is on vacation for his honeymoon and must return to England to take up a commission in the army. They demand to see his letter or telegram from the War Office re-calling him, which he does not have. On these occasions, I tell them that he is responding to a radio appeal that we all heard the day before. Fortunately, because my papers are all in order, and I have my laissez-passer from Sainte Maxime, they seem to believe me and let us through.

By now Reid's anxiety was causing him to drive at reckless speed whenever possible. My nerves were further challenged by the many accidents we passed along the way, and the myriad vehicles driven into ditches beside the road. One such was a heavy car that had been hit on the driving side, and the occupants forced to abandoned it. Another was a car, with a body lying dead across the torn radiator. We passed vehicles on fire, having hit trees, and many others overturned. Each time we approached such a scene I looked away, and found my eyes following the pine trees on the opposite side of the road. Had we suffered a puncture, I do not know how we would have fared, as there was nowhere to stop.

As it was, we seemed to be standing still, compared with the more powerful cars that sped past us, often on the wrong side of the road. Each time one was forced to slow down, male refugees tramping alongside the road ran forward and tried to board them, but they either fell off or were repelled. I never saw a single one succeed.

The afternoon was splendid as we approached our destination. I glimpsed the ocean sea through the trees, calm and blue, with white horses atop the waves. The Bay of Biscay was lovely after the thunderstorms, and there was a heady mix of ozone and scent from pine trees weeping resin.

We arrived about 6.30pm. Finding the Consulate closed, we wandered around looking for something to eat. Discovering a wee teashop, we ordered croissants, and I was allowed to have a wash in a pint of water in a bowl, my first since the evening before at the Salvation Army kitchen at Nîmes, and only the second time I had washed my face since I left Sainte Maxime. Following the drenching I had in Nîmes, my face was grimy, and stained in stripes by the dye from the green straw and bunch of geraniums on my hat.

The old panelled room – an embrasure built into the walls – was soothing and quiet, and the food was good, but I still felt ill from the bad coffee earlier. I did enjoy the tea and fresh milk. Refreshed, we agreed that Mr Reid, who knew Biarritz well, would go round the big hotels to see if they might have rooms where we could stay the night, while I took a walk to exercise my legs. We agreed to meet back at the car in an hour.

I walked down to the quay and saw a most imposing ship painted grey, standing high above the water. It had a pair of three-inch guns and looked most formidable. I went closer, and on the side I read 'Newhaven to Dieppe'. It was an old friend I had travelled on many times, yet now almost unrecognisable.

I stopped at a small bar and decided to take a cassis and soda. What a treat! And surely well-deserved after the journey I had had? Seated beside me were three young Poles who were talking of going to Portugal. Now that my promise to the Reids had been fulfilled, and I still had no visa to travel to England, I was free to go to the Watsons in Lisbon. So I told them that I was intending to go there in my car. They said that they had no French passports, and no means of transport, and would have to find their own way over the Pyrenees. I told them that, providing my visa did not come through for the boat to England, if they would take me with them, they could ride in my car, and I would meet any reasonable expenses up to 5,000 francs. We agreed to meet here again tomorrow evening at the same time to finalise our plans.

I was on my way back when I saw my car being driven towards me. Mr Reid had found a hotel with three single beds, someone having failed to return after booking earlier in the day. He drove us to a large hotel – Le Fevre – in impressive grounds overlooking the bay. In short order we were all in our rooms. I ordered a jug of boiling water to mix with the tinned milk and bread I had brought with me from Sainte Maxime. When none arrived, I used tap water and achieved a surprisingly good result. It proved as enjoyable a meal as I could have expected under the circumstances. When I had finished, I lay on a bed that seemed to me to be floating on clouds of swansdown, and in no time at all, I fell fast asleep.

Friday 21st June

At 6.45am I dressed, wrote up my diary, enjoyed another wash in hot running water, and went in search of breakfast. I was on the seventh floor and the lift was out of order. Eventually I found the breakfast room, where I had a coffee with milk and a piece of bread, and sent the Reids' breakfast up to their room.

I was anxious to leave, because although the Consulate did not open until 9am, I suspected that a dense crowd would already be there, as I had been told in the tea rooms yesterday that people had stood that day queuing for nine hours.

I went to Barclays Bank to change some of my money into Portuguese currency. Mr Reid came with me, because I had asked if he would send a wire to Bill telling him of my intention to try to leave for Portugal. I was alone in the bank except for an American lady and a well-dressed South African lady. While we waited, the American lady told me that a party had been arranged by the American Consul to have a special train to take them to Lisbon. She told me that it was easy to buy a pass-out visa at St Jean de Luz. The South African lady was sitting on a stool ahead of me. She had a long, long conversation with the cashier, which it was impossible for me not to overhear.

It transpired that she had angina pectoris and had engaged a taxi to take her and her maid from Paris to Lisbon. She was proving by her papers and marriage certificate that she was the wife of a millionaire – I think De Beers was the name – something to do with diamond mining[41]. She said that earlier she had sent her jewels to London, and all she wanted was 3,000 francs to pay her hotel bill and to buy a little petrol for the taxi. She continued her conversation for over 10 minutes but was ultimately refused because she wanted to pay in a cheque drawn against the Bank of Westminster. Crestfallen, she moved aside, and I took her place.

I changed my money with some difficulty as almost all of my English money was gone, except for £100 notes, and I had to keep the 5,000 francs that was allowed to leave the country.

As I turned to leave, the South African lady asked if I cared to take a cheque that I could cash on my arrival in England for my remaining English notes. I almost

---

[41] This is likely to have been Caroline Magdalen Oppenheimer, wife of Ernest Oppenheimer, chairman of De Beers from 1929. Her husband was helped by Ian Fleming and the Secret Service to flee to London with parcels of gems, together with Ernest Hemingway and other persons of note, from near Bordeaux in June 1940. The Oppenheimer family owned De Beers for 80 years until 2011.

consented but the instinct of self-preservation made me hesitate. I was still in France, with no transit visa out of France and into Spain, and when I did reach Lisbon, I might have to wait some time for a ship. And, if failing to get an exit visa from France, I knew that I would have to cross the Pyrenees on foot with the three Polish men. And so, with regret, I refused.

Mr Reid told me that he had sent the wire, and he was now going to the Consulate to get exit passes for a boat. We agreed to meet up again at the quay. Because I had determined to go via Spain and Portugal to preserve my car and possessions, I returned alone to the hotel.

When I arrived back at the hotel, I found people gathered around my car. They clamoured to persuade me to sell my car, but I refused them all. I was still convinced that I had made the right decision, and that even the mountains were preferable to being interned, as I hate crowds, and the thought of sleeping on straw. I shooed them away and drove down to the quay, where I saw that the boat had gone.

Presently the Reids arrived and took their cycles from the back of the car. I asked if they would take my little cabin trunk with them for safekeeping. They refused. Now that they had secured their passes for a ship, they had no interest in my plans. I saw that Mrs Reid had surreptitiously taken my two packets of Ryvita and had them beneath her arm. I demanded that she return them, which she did. Mr Reid scowled, saying, 'Take your damn car – people like you only think of themselves.'

I asked if this was how they treated their dressmaker and taxi drivers, but they simply cycled off without a backward glance.

I drove the car away from the quay to a quiet part of the town of Old Bayonne, and after locking it went to the Spanish Consulate. It was by now about 11am. I found myself standing in a dense mass, like a cup-tie crowd, except that here, people were desperate to save their lives. Most of these were Spanish people who had been living and working in France and were eager to return home. Some, however, were in real fear. As one young man said, 'If I am found by the Germans, I shall be taken prisoner and most probably shot!' He was a solicitor and asked if I would try to get him to the English Consulate, so that he might go to England. I tried as well as I could – his French was as limited as mine – to explain that if he had a trade or profession such as an engineer it might be possible, but not otherwise.

Another young man asked me the same question and I told him that I had heard it said that the BBC had made an appeal for French engineers to come to England, and that as he said he was a civil engineer, he should try the British Consul.

When I finally saw the Spanish Consul, he assured me that I could obtain a visa at once if bought through an agent in Rue d'Espagne at a cost of 1,000 francs. He gave me directions, and I left.

As I came away from him, in the crowd, I met the American lady I had seen at the bank this morning. She came to ask me if I could take her and her two friends to Lisbon, as the train could no longer be arranged. I told her that I was going to arrange a visa and I said that I would meet her tomorrow for lunch.

It was close to 5.30pm when I reached the tourist office in Rue d'Espagne. I was surprised to discover that the owner was English and just now that meant so much to me as 'British' was quite another thing – even the Reids were Scottish. He said that if I would leave my passport and the money, he would go himself in the morning to the Consul, because if he left now, by the time he got there, the Consul would have already left the bureau. I told him that I would come in the morning as I had a great fear of being parted from my passport for so long. He said in that case I should try our own Consul, who he felt sure could issue the necessary permit.

I went to the British Consulate, but it was closed. As I stood there wondering what to do, a Lancashire soldier came out and spoke to me. I asked him to ask by tomorrow if the next day it might be possible to go to Spain and Portugal with the aid of the Consul? He said he was with a military attaché from our embassy in Paris and pointed out their little camionette loaded outside. He said that if I am outside at 9am in the morning, he will personally take me in, rather than that I should wait in the crowd. I thanked him profusely and left.

I now had two tasks: to apologise to the Poles for having to let them down, and to find a bed for the night. I drove to the café where we met last evening to tell the young men that my plans were still uncertain, and I could not commit to take them. I do hope they are able to get clear, for I am certain that Hitler will have no mercy on young Poles.

I had been on my feet since early morning, and my legs ached. I ordered the same drink of cassis and soda and sat for a while until I felt fortified. It must have been about 7.30pm by now, and most of the shops were closed. Here in the old town, the shops were tiny, either up or down steps, not at all clean. Often there was no single product on offer, with wine, rabbit flesh, dried cod and cheap jewellery sold together, and always some wool. I found two shops open. In the first I bought, of all things, a piece of Lux, not expecting to find it here of all places. In the second shop I bought for tomorrow a piece of cheese – a luxury – although I had not eaten since breakfast at 7.30am.

I walked alone down the dark, winding and narrow streets. The people were speaking among themselves a language unintelligible to me – Basque, I presume. They seemed calm and cheerful, and untroubled by the war. I assume that for them, Bayonne and Biarritz will always be first and foremost tourist centres, and their only concern whether the season is good or bad.

By now I was very anxious. Apart from the cheese which I resolved to save and savour, I had no food, and no bed or shelter for the night. I came across a girl speaking French, who told me that she knew of a place with rooms for refugees. She led me to an old 1914 hospital, fitted up with 100 beds. As far as I could tell, it was clean and comfortable and had a large peaceful garden. I told the housekeeper that I had no need of charity and would happily pay hotel prices for a bed, if I could lie down straight away. She that I must go first to receive a ticket from the Refugee Centre at the railway station.

There was no bus and the streets were cordoned off from traffic because of the crowds. I walked a mile or so to the station. There were hundreds of poor people, representing every European country, sitting on their belongings in a large enclosed station yard, many with children and babes in arms, waiting patiently. I asked a group of five where they were going; they said 'America'. Many had hardly any luggage, just a package each and a cotton blanket. I understood now why there were no beds available in the town. And after all that, the Refugee Centre was closed!

I trudged back to the car in the dark and the rain, too weary to attempt an impossible search for a room. I was very tired and anxious, and muddled about where I had left it. I had been to so many places with it over the past 24hrs. Time and again I arrived at a street where I thought I had left it, to no avail.

I walked again and again through the maze of streets in the old town, with rows of cars down one side of every street, so many of which seemed just like mine, until I came close. I became increasingly convinced that it had been stolen.

Unable to walk another step, I leaned against the bonnet of a car, and flagged down a British soldier on a bicycle. I asked him if he would cycle through the surrounding streets, looking for a buff-coloured car marked GW 400 and bearing a GB badge. He and his friend told me to meet them outside the butcher's shop in half an hour.

Twenty minutes later he came saying they had searched every single street and it was nowhere to be found. I thanked them and wanted to give them something for their pains, but they refused, wished me luck, and cycled away.

I walked weary and downcast along one of the main streets of old Bayonne that led down to the quay, in the hope that I might at least find a café there. On reaching the bottom of the street where it emerged onto the quay, I saw the car. My delight overcame my weariness. I hurried to it to unlock the door and sat inside while I decided what to do next.

I began by writing down the name of the street – Rue Bernadou – on the back of an envelope. I wondered if it was Provençal – like Lou Roustidou – or Basque. It mattered not, as later when I asked for directions back to my car, no one had even heard of it! I took off my shoes, wrapped myself in a rug, and tried to sleep.

Saturday 22nd June – Morning

I had a restless night and dozed a little, when at around 4 o'clock I was woken by the sound of market people beginning to arrive, the wheels of the barrows on the cobbles more effective than any alarm. A man approached, pushing such a barrow laden with fruit. I espied bananas, bought ten, and ate two, thinking the others would make a nice hoard as I knew they were likely to be the last I might have for some time.

A lady passed by eating cherries. She was miserably wet, cold and dishevelled, looking as though she had been out in the open all night. We greeted each other. She said the cherries were her first meal since yesterday morning and asked where I had found the bananas? I sent her hurrying down the street after the man with the barrow.

Feeling revived by the food, I started to hunt for a bed so that I might have a few hours' good sleep. I began asking passers-by if they knew of anywhere where I might sleep and get a little food, saying I would willingly pay for the trouble. The reply of one girl was typical of most. She said it was the same for her and her friends. They were without food except for a few dried things. It was ironic that here we were, surrounded by handcarts laden with fruit and vegetables and rabbits, and yet there was nothing else that we could readily eat. Eventually I was told to move on as my car was blocking the market, and I realised that it was now the only one in the street.

I started the car but was hemmed in by stalls and handcarts and was unable to move forwards or backwards. When I asked for assistance, nobody understood my French, nor I them. I finally found a kindly-looking man who agreed to get me out. He began arranging vehicles behind me, horses, donkeys and human beings, and then reversed adroitly down to the end of the street. I thanked him, and then went back up the street on foot with a can, in search of water for my radiator.

I walked amongst plump rabbits in cages, poor things. They were quite fearless, having been hand-reared and petted, and quite oblivious to their fate. There were also the most beautiful peaches, apricots and strawberries. Lovely vegetables of all kinds and all colours. Sliced boiled beet and aubergines, large red peppers, bleached endive, and other yellow things amongst the green. Overhead, the brilliant sunshine and blue sky were accentuated after a night of thunder and lightning and torrential downpours. I felt like Noah taking his first step from the ark.

I found a water fountain on the quay, where the mouth of the river ran down to the sea. It was swollen, in full flood from the storm. I watched, mesmerised by the muddy brown water carrying branches and other debris, tumbling wildly towards the ocean. After what seemed an age, I tore myself away and returned to the car. Since it was too early to return to the Consulate, I sat and watched the market, bustling with sellers and buyers.

At about 6am, I went in search of breakfast. I wandered through the old town, losing myself in the narrow streets and alleys, indistinguishable one from another. The two cafés that I came across were full and the doors locked. A local woman saw me standing outside one of them, staring through the window with what must have seemed a despondent stare, and advised me to go to the market I had left three quarters of an hour ago, where she said I was sure to find a café open!

I trudged back to the market and found that the cafés that had been closed were now open and doing brisk business. I ordered and drank two cups of barley effusion, well fortified with some of the tinned milk I had brought in from the car, and greedily devoured a hunk of bread. When I had finished, I asked a waiter if I could wash my hands. He led me to the sink, where I took my bar of Lux from my coat pocket and turned on the tap. My hands were still covered in soap when the proprietress stormed angrily into the kitchen, demanding to know how I thought she could carry on her business if her kitchen was full of customers washing in her sink? She told me to leave immediately.

I returned to my car and, not for the first time, was thankful for my hoard of unused paper serviettes that I had collected over the winter in Provence.

At 7am I went to the Consulate and took up my stand so that I could lean on the little British Embassy camionette and wait for the opening. There were already hundreds of people on either side of the door. There was a notice on the wall:

'It is recommended to take 48 hours of food to the boat.'

Now I understood why Mrs Reid had attempted to leave with my packets of Ryvita under her arm, both of which I took from her. The Reids must have seen the notice when they came for their passes. On the right of the door was another notice proclaiming:

'British Subjects Only.'

It found it difficult to believe my eyes, given all of the different nations represented in the queues. There were people from every nation across Europe and every continent. I gathered that most of the women, accompanied by children, were wives of British citizens. Others came from the colonies. But all, it seemed, took precedence over us 'Islanders' and were totally without scruple in obtaining entrance out of turn. If a messenger went through the door, immediately the queue dissolved as people besieged him, waving notes to take to the Consul. The young, strong men worked their way forward by crushing others out of their paths with their elbows.

A French soldier approached and insisted that I take a place at the end of the queue. I said that I was waiting for a messenger, and had a message to give to the Consul, and he had a message for me. I explained that I was here by arrangement, waiting for the soldier I had seen the night before to come and fetch me. But he would have none of it, and took me by the arm and pushed me down the street.

As soon as his back was turned, I made my way back to lean on the camionette. But each time I did this, he would shout '*Dame au chapeau!*' at me, grab my arm, and drag me to the back of the queue. I suppose he was only doing his duty, but our game of tug of war continued until at about 10.30am, the soldier appeared and beckoned me to join him in the doorway.

The Consul from Pau had just arrived, he told me, to relieve the Pro-Consul. Two people were sitting at a table stamping passports. The Consul was standing behind them. He asked me why I wanted to go to Lisbon and said that he could get me an exit visa for Spain if I came back at 2pm, however he strongly recommended that I board the ship tomorrow morning and go direct to

England. He explained that the news was not favourable. Germany was pressing Spain to refuse transit visas, and Portugal was in fear of Germany attacking though Spain. Times were uncertain, he said, and things could change overnight.

I told him that I had travelled with two English people who had gone by boat yesterday, but that I did not have a ticket for the boat. He immediately offered me a ticket. With but a moment's hesitation, I took it. I asked if I might be allowed to sit for a while. The Lancashire soldier took me over to a chair where he had left his bag and satchel and placed them on the floor so that I could sit down. I rested there for an hour.

Presently a young man, another Lancashire soldier, was brought to sit near me. He was wearing a civilian overcoat over hospital pyjamas and was sockless in a pair of old slippers. He told me that he had been wounded and taken to a hospital in Paris. When the Germans approached the city, he had managed to get a lift from the military attaché all the way here. He was quite jolly and smoked one cigarette after another. He said he had made lots of mates here with strangers who had become separated from the rest of their units.

I left with my head in a whirl, clutching my boat ticket. I knew that I would have to abandon my car and was much grieved at this. I still am. Will had showered it with love. Checking the oil, the water and petrol every day, and kicking the tyres each night to say 'goodnight'! At St Paul, he had a constant running battle to keep boys from scratching their names on it. The car has become very dear to me, and now I must leave it here on foreign soil. I feel as though I am leaving a faithful horse who has brought me here safely, and without complaint. I also sense that I am letting Will down – Will, who had treasured it so and prepared it meticulously for our journey. A preparation that had cost him his life.

What makes it worse is knowing that I could have reached Lisbon, with all our goods intact, but for agreeing to bring the Reids to Bordeaux. I confess, I am still uncertain as to the wisdom of using the boat ticket.

By now, each side of the street was filling with people clamouring to get into the Consulate. I was accosted many times by foreigners begging me to try and get them to England. I said I could not. There were thousands who were waiting their turn, and there would be many more. Many of these people had no claim whatsoever to come to England but were desperate to leave France. I tried to explain how small England was and how our food was all imported. That the German navy and submarines were bombarding us already, and we had many more people than France, which was six times as big.

I managed to escape and went to the quay, where I joined a queue outside a restaurant. Presently I was handed a plate, sat down and was delighted to find there was stew, and hot soup, with pieces of rabbit and all sorts of vegetables. The tureen was brought round, and I helped myself liberally.

I wrote another note to Bill about Reid, to go with the contract that I intend to post to him before I leave and went to the car. I was closing the roof when a French officer, seeing GB plates, came to help me. He then asked if I would care to exchange my francs for some £1 notes. I was pleased do so now that I was about to leave.

He said he had just come from England, where they were expecting an invasion and were rapidly building fortresses along the coast. He offered me 30 notes for my francs, and I asked if they were really English as they looked so new and green and in a new print I have not seen before. He said, 'Yes, they are English. New notes. If you don't want them, don't take them.'

I gave him 175 francs for each.

Now I was faced with packing all of my belongings into boxes or other containers I might take on the ship or send to England. But I had none. I was standing there wondering what to do, when an English soldier asked if he could help. I explained, and he offered to drive me down to the quay where I might be able to buy some.

When we arrived, the routes into the town were now barricaded with ropes and the car must be left outside. But there were buildings along the quay that serviced the boats and ships that I thought might have what I was seeking. The soldier offered to stay with the car to guard my belongings while I set off on my search.

I entered a ship's chandler, a chemist, several grocery shops, but none of them had anything suitable that I might buy, not even empty cartons or brown paper. I had almost despaired when I saw a man carrying a basket like a large square fruit hamper with a lid. I went over to ask where he had bought it. He told me that it was a place on the far side of the Old Town, and when I told the soldier, he said that if I would give him some money, he would go and purchase several.

Twenty minutes later, he returned empty-handed, saying they had all been sold. Nor was there even any string with which to bundle up my possessions. We went back into town together, and just as I was giving up hope of finding anything, I saw a shop with its display window missing. Inside the shop, a girl was sweeping, and in one corner of the room was a large trunk. I asked to see it. There was no price on it, and she declared that in any case she could not sell it to me. I offered increasing amounts of money for it, eventually as high as 150 francs as I saw I must buy it. She steadily refused, saying that the patron had told her not to sell anything as they were closing down. She told me where she thought I could buy some string at a seedsman on the quay, and the soldier and I hurried back the way we had come.

There we found some good thick cord, which I purchased. I asked the proprietor why all of the shops were closing, and he told me that perishables were being sold, as money was changing from francs to marks, with 100 francs equalling 4 marks, and they had been told that nothing more must be offered. We took the cord back to the car and the soldier went to the Consulate to see if there was any news of a ship.

He returned, saying that people were coming out with their tickets for a boat, saying they were going to the quay, even though we had just left there, and we knew there was no ship in harbour. He said they had been told to be patient.

My soldier and I began to empty the car. A young Frenchman came forward and offered to help. He and the soldier began to cut up the green tarpaulin that Will had placed over our belongings and set about using it to create large bundles. While they worked, I addressed a dozen labels I had just bought in the seedsman's, together with pens and ink.

Then I went through Will's papers, many and varied, brought with us from Cambridge. He had kept everything! Letters from people I had never heard of, receipts and all manner of trivial things, heaps of letters that I knew I ought to keep. There were copies of our leases, current and out of date agreements. I was concerned that I might lose them if our ship was sunk, as I had learned had happened to the last boat to depart Bordeaux. I decided to place them in envelopes and mail them to Bill. I labelled these and placed them on the bonnet while I supervised the lacing up of the sheet into two large sausages tied with thick string and straps that the men had magicked from somewhere.

While we were thus engaged, lots of people had stopped to watch, forming quite a crowd. As we finished, they began to disperse, and then I discovered that my beautiful sealskin coat that I had left on the passenger seat was gone! I had a moment's anger and sense of loss, and then I reminded myself that all of our values have altered now. What was value before – sealskin coats, typewriters, cars – is no longer important. Our safety comes first.

I thanked the young Frenchman, and told him he was like an English Gentleman, which he took as a compliment. My soldier offered to drive me to the post office and I readily accepted. He seems determined to stick by me, and as he also has a ticket for a boat, it makes good sense.

I tried to send some of my money home for safekeeping by registered letter, but was told that it was forbidden to send money out of the country. I hastily wrote a short note to Bill, giving a calmer explanation of my agreement with Reid that I was enclosing, and made suitable packets in large envelopes taken from old letters, and sent Will's most important papers by airmail. All of these were registered. I also enclosed the money, which must take its luck as, if it is opened, I know it will be confiscated.

Saturday 22nd June – Afternoon

I will never forget this day. At around 4pm, I asked a man whose wife had allowed me to rest in her car for a little while, what he was going to do with their car. He said that he had made arrangements to leave it in an International garage at 100 francs a month until the war is over. He felt sure that it would be safe. But he was an American – I think, perhaps, that with me it might be different. With my GB plates, and the fact that it will be known that the owner is English, I believe it likely that it will be confiscated.

We drove the car down to the quay so that we might place my luggage ready to board whatever boat might arrive. A Dutch boat – the *Queen Emma* – was already leaving, its decks packed with military folk, mainly Czechs and Poles, who had been given priority tickets earlier. We were told that it was not the best of refugee boats, as there were no beds on board and no food.

My car was now surrounded by people making offers to purchase it. Each time I named a price, they said that was too dear as it was necessary to pay import duty here, or on entering Spain. One couple said that if I would write a receipt for a few hundred francs – which they showed me – they would watch the car for me in case I needed suddenly to use it. I realised that I would be making a gift of it and that as soon as my back was turned, they would drive it away. I was in a quandary, as I knew that a car had to be accompanied – hence their request for a receipt – because the customs officers were busy clearing the streets of the multitude of abandoned cars. Luckily for me, before I had to make this difficult decision, there was a general stampede from the quay. People were calling taxis and rushing off with their luggage. I asked the soldier to inquire what was happening.

He returned, saying that word had been sent from the Consulate that a boat was due in St Jean de Luz at 5pm. He carried my luggage back to the car as I dared not leave it, for fear of it being stolen. A ring of people had now gathered around to rush onto it. We threw the stuff in, and started for the ship at full speed, so thankful that the car had not been garaged or sold.

Despite the rush of cars and taxis, we covered the 14 miles at a speed of 40 miles an hour and were able to find a parking space not 50 yards from the quay. Luggage was already piling up, and I was directed to leave my two carefully labelled tarpaulin sausages with all the rest. I left the car in the soldier's care, and he watched the remainder of my luggage while I tried to find something to eat. I decided to save my packet of Ryvita and the bananas, as I was still a long way from England and the boat might yet fail to arrive. I bought a bottle of Vichy water, drank it all, and returned to the car. My soldier left me now to make friends with other English soldiers. I shall miss him.

A Frenchwoman came to ask if she might help me to unload, but I refused. I knew that if I left the car for a moment it would be driven away with all its contents, as had happened to others. I used the time to stitch a pocket of cloth inside my coat with a darning needle and some crochet cotton, where I will keep my money and passport safe. I also made a sort of pillowcase to hold my toilet things, and nightdress, medicine, bananas, and tins of milk and Ryvita. I intend to throw it over my shoulder, leaving my hand free for my small cabin trunk – the one Reid had refused to take.

Suddenly I became aware of people moving towards the quay. I got out of the car and saw that the ship had arrived and was at anchor outside the harbour. I gathered my belongings, bade farewell to my precious car and hurried to the quay.

The British Navy had chartered ninety large flat 'sardine' boats to take us to the ship – a real liner with two main decks besides the staff deck. We were told to move forward to the boats and leave the luggage where it was to be collected later. I had my pillowcase tied securely to my body, two handbags on my forearm, and my case in my right hand.

Hundreds of us seemed to move as one, jammed together as we made the perilous descent down steep, slippery steps to the sea. It was cruel to bear. Children were screaming, hurt by the crush; burly Basque porters forced their way through the crowd, and rushed up and down the steps. A naval officer, trying to bring a semblance of order, told me to leave my case at the top of the stairs. When I hesitated, he said,

'You cannot possibly take all that up the stepladder to board the ship. Have no fear, the whole quay will be cleared, and everything brought to the *Ettrick*[42] when people are aboard.'

I was halfway down the steps when I realised that the beautiful morocco leather bag, my last birthday gift from Will, was no longer on my arm. It was made of

[42] Built in 1938, the *Ettrick* was a P&O liner requisitioned by the British Government as a troop carrier. It was sunk by a U-boat en route to Glasgow from Gibraltar in 1942.

beautiful black pigskin lined with grey suede and had many useful pockets. Inside I had stowed some colourful silk scarves I had bought in Nîmes as gifts, a bracelet I had removed from my wrist for safety, and, I fear, my driving licence. I can only assume that it must have been cut off by a neighbour in the crowd. Ah well!

The huge flat sardine boat was bucking up and down on the swell. As I clambered in, I was thrown to my knees. Here suddenly was the real Biscay – pelting rain and very stormy. I managed to turn over and ended up sitting with my back against the side. It was then that I realised that my pillowcase was also gone.

The boat filled rapidly until there were thirty of us crammed together, and the man at the tiller swung us away from the steps, knocking a lady's hat off in the process, scattering her things about her. As the boat turned into the mountainous waves, the prow bucked up and down like a wild horse at a rodeo. A youth stood in the bows, holding a formidable boathook, watching to see which of us would be the first to fall overboard.

Immediately below him sat a curious party. A middle-aged man with a moustache, wearing a heavy woollen overcoat and a trilby hat, accompanied by a woman, a young girl, and three or four servants. What distinguished them from the rest of us was that they appeared to have been allowed to bring with them a considerable number of japanned boxes. The lady next to me saw me staring and whispered, 'That is King Zog, his wife and child.'

Poor old King Zog of Albania[43], exiled by Mussolini,

---

[43] Originally the prime minister, then dictatorial president, King Zog the First was proclaimed monarch with Italian support in 1928. He suppressed civil liberties, but did end serfdom, introduced primary education for all, and banned cruelty to animals. He and his people also offered refuge to any Jew seeking shelter from Nazi harassment. Zog survived over fifty assassination attempts, but in 1939 Mussolini invaded Albania and forced the King into exile. He spent his later years in France up to his death in 1961, having never again been permitted to set foot in his own country.

and forced to seek a home in Europe. And now, here he was in this wretched little boat with me, just another refugee tossed about by the cruel sea. I recalled that there had been reports in the London *Times* that he had fled with all of the country's gold reserves. I could not help wondering if that was what was in those boxes.

Our boat had reached the ship, where it was alternately thrown against the hull and sucked back by the waves. We were required to climb a loose ladder – with a moveable handrail each side – lowered from the deck some twenty steps above us. King Zog's party was the first to be invited to go aboard. One of his retinue was close behind the King, ensuring he did not fall. The other helpers followed his wife and child, each of them struggling to carry one of the boxes.

When it came to my turn, two sailors lifted me onto a suspended platform a yard square. The boat made a great heave, and I was helped by its fall onto the first rung of the ladder which I mounted on my hands and knees, not daring to hold the handrail rope in case my fingers were grazed against the hull. Someone was helping by pushing me from behind. I was conscious of angry, dark waters beneath me, wet and cold, and the spray striking my cheeks like hailstones.

When they hauled me up through the gates onto the deck, a great feeling of relief washed over me, and I now understood why the officer had ordered me to leave my belongings on the wharf. There was no way in which I could have managed to board, encumbered by all my luggage. I was directed to the dining room, where I was told the purser would allocate me a room.

In the dining room, there was a sense of calm and order, and I was unable to sense the movement of the ship that had been so evident on deck. I was among the first to board and was able to go straight to the purser to ask for a berth number. He said, 'I am sure you are tired; you should go and lie down.'

I had no difficulty finding my berth but there was already a lady making herself at home. I told her that I had just been allocated this berth. She smiled and said, 'First come, first served!'

When I asked her name, she replied curtly, 'Mrs Fullerton, not that it is any concern of yours.'

I returned to the dining room and told the purser that my berth was already occupied. He asked me to go and tell Mrs Fullerton that she must come up and see him so that he might arrange the matter. Before I went, I asked if I might have a settee or something other than a top berth because of my bad knees, which have been much aggravated by the last few days. He immediately gave me another berth, which turned out to be an even better and larger cabin. I was to share it with a Jewish lady. I flung my coat on the settee and, having nothing else with me, lay down on my bunk. I had been undressed only partly since I left Sainte Maxime and now, because of fear that we might be torpedoed, I resolved to sleep fully dressed until we reached England.

Sunday 23rd June

When I awoke this morning, I had no idea of the time. It seemed as though years had passed since I last lay this long without moving. In fact, it had been six days with little or no sleep – with the exception of the night in the hotel in Biarritz – feeling exhausted all the time and in a permanent state of anxiety. I lay for a long time daydreaming, then there came a knock on our door. It was a very distinguished English lady with white hair, from the British Red Cross. She said did I know it was 1 o'clock in the afternoon, and that since I had missed breakfast and lunch, would I like some hot tea and a piece of freshly made cake? She and her companions were going from compartment to compartment with these treats, and even had milk for the children. I cannot tell you how overwhelmed I was to have been so well received after such a terrible journey. I confess that I cried. And so, I suspect, did she.

Once refreshed, I made my way to the lounge, where many people had gathered. I sat next to a girl, about twenty-five years of age. Her name was Lizzy, and she had come from St Nazaire. She told me that she had been staying with the Consul, who had no means of getting away except by taking somebody else's car from a garage and loading his office stuff into it. She had been shopping with friends and had just returned as he was ready to leave. He told her she had just five minutes and no more to get her things together as he was leaving immediately. She had a handbag and mackintosh, but no coat. As they were about to set off, a man came up saying he was from the Consulate in Paris and wanted to go to England, and did they have room for him? They did not, but by some miracle he had appeared on our ship. He had been well prepared, having thrown everything away, even his coat, and had finished the last part of his journey on foot, and had not even a coat!

Lizzy said that the afternoon before their departure from St Nazaire, they saw a beautiful ship[44] which had just left harbour. It looked as though it must have struck a mine, as a great waterspout was thrown up, and it sank almost at once, no person getting away. She said that night was inky black and raining torrents, and crowds were still waiting to leave the quay. This did nothing to dispel my concerns about our being torpedoed!

I asked if my companions would save my place for me if I had a little walk to stretch my legs. I completed

---

[44] At 3.45pm, on 17th June 1940, the RMS *Lancastria*, a converted liner, had just finished loading some 6,000 troops and refugees when she was struck by three or four bombs from a single German bomber. The boat keeled over, trapping many below the waterline. With so many on board, there were too few lifeboats. German planes strafed the survivors and dropped flares onto the oil seeping from the vessel. Many were burned alive. Approximately 2,500 people were rescued, but over 3,500 were killed, including women and children. The event remains the single greatest loss of life in British maritime history.

several circuits of the lounge and the second-class dining room. Pausing at one of the windows in the corridor between the two, I spied another ship[45], much larger than ours, taking on board many troops. A steward told me they were members of the Polish Army and Air Force as well as any remaining British refugees.

Whilst passing through the dining room, I had noticed that they were very nearly ready to serve supper, it being close to 6.30pm. I informed Lizzy and my other companions, and they said we should head there straight away as the queues were long and acted like a pack of hounds scrapping after every last bone.

And so it proved. Self-important-looking men with medals on show – either for safety, or to demonstrate their worth – hung onto the coat-tails of the stewards as they passed by, in an attempt to get to the head of the queue, quite out of turn. So-called 'ladies' barged in front of mothers standing patiently with their children by their side. I had already formed the opinion that if you wish to see the best and worst of humankind, then look no further than a war.

The service staff were Arabs of some sort, spoke little English, and did not understand French. But they knew their work and we soon found one polite word in English brought immediate results. We had soup, sausage and mash, cold meat and salad, and sweets or a pot of tea or bread, butter and jam for supper. After the privations of the past many days, I could barely believe my eyes. Both the quality and quantity were excellent, and yet there were people who lifted the food up, smelled it, and made rude remarks! These were the same people who left their shoes outside their cabins, expecting someone to clean them for them.

After supper, we returned together to the lounge. There I met another girl from Biarritz. The niece of the

---

[45] Built in 1927, the SS *Arandora Star*, was a British Blue Star Line ocean liner and cargo ship. In 1929 she became a cruise ship. At the outbreak of war, she was requisitioned as a troopship.

Dean of Lichfield, she had taken a degree in London in psychology and had taught and taken a post as governess to the only son of the richest people in America. She claimed that when she started, he was painfully shy and virtually illiterate, but that after four years he was quite at ease with people and almost a genius. She was greatly relieved as she and her companions had only just caught the boat. With me she was like a lady nurse, often giving me well-prepared sandwiches of her own, and fruit between meals. On the settee opposite was an English lady who had been managing a hostel for dancers at the Folies Bergère in Paris. She had brought up two French girls as her own, and when the Germans came, she had had to leave them and the house which she owned. Beside her was a middle-aged French lady with her English husband. They were an odd couple. His wife was complaining about his not having shoes and blamed their maid. Not wanting to be transplanted in England, they seemed almost ready to return to Paris, apparently unaware that it was under German occupation.

We chatted and whiled away the night, nobody wishing to go to bed, and all of our sleep patterns gone awry. At about 4.40am, a Jewess and her husband came into the lounge, completely soaked, and carrying two wet handbags. They had just come aboard in the middle of a downpour of which we had been completely unaware. We directed them to the nearest bathroom. I decided it was time I went to my berth, where I soon fell asleep.

Monday 24th June

When I woke, it was only 6.30am, but knowing that I would not get back to sleep, I went out to see if there were any baths nearby. I met a steward who was bringing to each of the cabins a tiny piece of soap wrapped in paper. I asked if it were possible to have a little refreshment. He went to see and was soon back. He regretted that the kitchen was closed. The cook, he said, was a very large Englishman and had his hours. He then told me that the nearest bathroom with a bath would be ready at 10am, but as there are 8,000 people on board, I should never get a bath. He said he had only lain down for an hour last night as thousands were soaked from arriving in the sardine boats and staff were occupied.

When I told him that I had not had a wash for two days, he said, 'Oh dear! Please wait here.' He hurried away and soon returned with the key to the bathroom, and a large towel. While I waited, he turned on taps as big as fire engine taps, that filled the bath with sea water, and then brought fresh water in a bowl so that I might rinse afterwards. Oh, what a luxury!

Here everything is of supreme cleanliness and perfection. I have not been in a ship for nearly 20 years, and the luxury and size of my cabin and berth amazed me, with its wardrobe, two fitted large basins and plenty of hanging pegs, and any amount of fresh air on opening the portholes. And the ship is of such a size that although there are so many aboard, and many lying on the floors, there is no sense of overcrowding.

I hurried back to tell the others about the bath and went to breakfast. I had a wonderful meal of porridge, egg and bacon, and butter and marmalade with new bread. There are also boiled eggs, but I was told that they are not so nice – very small and tasting of packing. The milk is dried and diluted, but the service is excellent. The little foreign stewards move quickly and almost imperceptibly, and if anything is asked for, it is brought immediately, and they are always anxious to serve.

After breakfast, I set out on a tour of the deck to find my luggage, which my steward said had been brought on at 6am. This was a gorgeous midsummer's morning, very warm, with a clear blue sky and tranquil sea. People were still arriving in sardine boats – aptly named, given the number of bodies packed into them. On the seaward side of the boat, I came upon the luggage. Never was there such baggage! There had been a downpour all night and the not so strong had burst, and all kinds of things were squeezing out from under the tons of wetness. Blue boxes were grey, all had been heaped together and were shapeless, even the real leather. It must have been heaped and waiting for hours, waiting to be lowered to the boat and the weight had distorted the shape.

The Jewish lady from my cabin was looking for a hatbox. She found it with the lid missing. She was very disappointed. It had contained several pairs of shoes, and now only two odd shoes remained. The soldier who drove the Embassy camionette from Paris to the Consulate was also there. He said that he had lost four Remington typewriters. As his luggage had been near mine on the quay, and I could see none of it, we went together to the purser to complain about our lost property. An officer told us that a guard was mounted from a destroyer with drawn bayonets and had never left it, and that it must be somewhere. Some had gone in the hold. We went there, but his and mine were still missing. The same officer said it must be on the other ship that was being convoyed with us, the *Arandora Star*. I hope I will be able to find it when we arrive in England.

This morning, there was a hive of activity on board. Some of the ladies decided to organise ways of helping improve conditions on the ship. A whole nursing unit of 25 British nurses and their drivers were on board. I discovered that their leader was called Mary Spears[46], and she had formed this Anglo-French unit to support the French Army in Eastern France until they were forced

---

[46] Mary Spears was a successful American-born novelist, known by her maiden name as Mary Borden. Spears was her surname by her second marriage to a brigadier general, whom she had met while running a frontline field hospital during WWI. After being forced to abandon her outpost in France in 1940, she raised new funds and then led her unit to support the Free French fighting under De Gaulle in the Middle East in 1941.

to retreat by the Germans. The nurses had to flee south and having split from their French colleagues, arrived here in St Jean de Luz on the same ship as King Zog, with nothing but their personal possessions. They began to see to the sick among us.

Some swept the communal rooms, while others waited on those unable to get around freely, or busied themselves trying to soothe the less fortunate, by making them comfortable. Those of us lucky enough to have cabins were asked to share spare blankets and pillows with those sleeping in the communal areas, or to arrange to vacate our berths during the day, so that people using deckchairs or lying on the floor could lie down to stretch themselves. I had two people who came regularly to us.

One was a Yorkshire lady recovering from pneumonia who was very feeble. The other was a woman who suffered a great deal from seasickness and was tied to her baby. I asked my steward to arrange a bath for her. She was found a bath later. The Jewish man whose wife was in the berth above me came each morning, stripped to the waist to wash and shave. Her husband slept with hundreds of others in hammocks forward. I believe they were very comfortable, and they waited on themselves. She also took in an American woman who wanted to bring in her boy of 14 years, who had some developmental disorder, to sleep on the floor when other people wouldn't hear of it.

We had boiled beef for lunch today, with potatoes mashed in their skins, and greens. Due to the numbers of people, service was a little slow, and when it was suggested to one man that he should help bring the food from the kitchen, he refused, saying his son was a major! Everyone roared with laughter. I confess, I joined in too.

After lunch, in the lounge, I sat beside the American woman. She confided that she had been married to an Englishman in the army years ago and was now divorced. She said that her boy was her life, but she didn't know what she was going to do with him in

England. I suggested that during wartime, boarding school was probably best. We soon became firm friends.

The Jewish lady came to join us. She missed her comfortable flat in Paris, which was now being enjoyed by the women who had been her maids, while here was she on this refugee boat. She gave her husband much grief by constantly saying that they were fools to have left Paris. I wondered how she could possibly think that when there were so many Jewish people on this boat from all over Europe, who had fled the Germans because of how they were treated? But she was so adamant that I kept my thoughts to myself. She asked my opinion on where it might be best for them to stay in England, saying that they thought that Cumberland might be safest. I told them that Cumberland was a centre for bombing on account of the Vickers shipyard in Barrow, so they decided to go and stay at the Grosvenor, where they were in the habit of going. If that was not safe, she thought they might try for America.

The talk then turned to how we might keep ourselves busy and assist those less fortunate than ourselves. We came up with the notion of organising language classes. I went immediately to speak with some of the Polish officers. They thought it a wonderful idea. And in no time at all, between us we had organised three classes a day. They all spoke fluent French and had marvellous English accents. When I asked how that came about, they said that they learned the phonetics so that they would be able to order things, buy food, get shaved and washed, seek help if lost, and a heap of useful things.

We had no paper or books, and it was very taxing and stretched one's memory, due to the great variety of those who came to our classes. But everyone was so hopeful, and very cheerful. We had sing-songs, where different nationalities took it in turn to teach the rest a song. We clapped heartily with the Czechs and Poles, but the French effort – the Marseillaise – went flat and was quickly dropped. The Poles, like the Welsh, were born to sing, so full of passion and emotion, and when I heard the translations, it brought tears to my eyes.

One of our fellow teachers was the lady who had been almost unbelievably kind to me when she came first to the cabin and found me so exhausted, feeding me with her own good food. It transpired that she was a niece to the Dean of Lichfield and had often been to Girton during Barbara's time there. I shall be going to bed this evening very tired, but both gratified and content for the first time since Will passed away.

Tuesday 25th June

Today our lessons continued apace, becoming ever more popular. In between classes, I met all manner of interesting people. And on a ship like ours, one's neighbours became very friendly.

By an amazing coincidence, on our table at lunch were some people from Bolton. I asked if they knew Threlfall Engineers in Salop Street in Bolton. The husband laughed, and said he knew it very well indeed. He had served his time there as an apprentice! He now had an oil and petrol depot in Paris but had kept up his friendship with Bolton. I told him that one of my sisters was Mrs Hurst, the wife of Robert Augustus Hurst, the owner, and that Threlfall had been the original name of the firm.

Another family had come from Angers in the Loire, where the father worked in the Polish Government quarters[47]. It had been heavily bombed, and the offices were moved to London. The father of the family had not been able to get the necessary exit visa, had no car, and there were no trains or transport. In order that they might escape to a place of safety and make their way to

---

[47] Angers was from December 1939 to June 1940 the home of the Polish government in exile, following the German occupation of Poland. Thereafter, it was based in London until 1990, when it recognised Lech Walesa as the first non-Communist president of Poland.

London, he had bought a coal lorry together with its contents, and paid a man with a driving licence and all the necessary papers, to drive them to Bordeaux, and then to St Jean de Luz. They had arrived black with coal dust, and just in time for the boat. They told me that while they were waiting on the quay, a Boy Scout had cycled up, saying that he had come a long way to ask the officers for help to fetch some poor unfortunate boys who were trying to make their way there without the means of transport and who were on foot. I pray that they made it, and that they are on this ship or on the *Arandora Star*.

This evening, King Zog, his wife and child sat at a table by themselves, right next to us.[48]

Notwithstanding the conditions we are all under, they are a very glamorous couple: he in his double-breasted worsted suit, she in a black twinset with a matching bow in her hair and a pearl necklace. The child – a boy, I think –who can be no more than eighteen months old, sat beside his mother in a high chair, accompanied by a maid. Queen Geraldine is very beautiful, and at least twenty years younger than him, although he is still handsome for a man of his age. There is something of a resemblance to the actor William Powell[49], I think. Unfortunately, he smoked one cigarette after another throughout the meal, his cigarette in an ebony holder, and the smoke wafting in our direction[50].

[48] King Zog's party fled south to Bordeaux, where the British military attaché sent them to a villa outside the town of Arcachon, where a British naval lieutenant, one Ian Fleming, was waiting for them. He arranged for them to board HMS *Galatea* which sailed to St Jean de Luz, where they boarded Kate's ship. The creator of James Bond was a member of the Royal Navy's Naval Intelligence Department, with the codename '17F', and shortly after this was promoted to Lieutenant Commander. He proposed a number of unusual schemes before forming a field intelligence unit, 30 Commando Unit, whose operations he initially directed from the safety of his desk at the Admiralty.

[49] No relation to Kate's husband, Will Powell, but an MGM star in Hollywood, married for a time to Carole Lombard, and later the partner of Jean Harlow. He died in 1984 at the age of 91.

Wednesday 26th June

Today was much the same as yesterday. Breakfast, lunch, supper, and in between we carried on our classes, which have become so popular that there is barely room for people to stand.

I was beginning to think that we would never arrive, but at 5.50 this evening, together with our Royal Navy escort, we slipped into Plymouth harbour! The cheers, the clapping and people singing in so many different languages will remain in my memory forever. But pride of place must go to the moment when everyone joined in singing 'God Save The King'!

We were told that we must stay on board until the morning. I am so excited that I wonder if I will sleep tonight?

Thursday 27th June

Up early and no breakfast this morning, but instead we disembarked! We were overjoyed and overwhelmed by the welcome from women of the WVS[51] who had cauldrons of tea and sandwiches waiting for us. We sat on benches and laughed and chatted as we ate and drank.

Having made so many friends, there were a great deal of goodbyes to be made, some it quite sad and tearful. There were many people for whom this was a foreign land, and had come without friends or relatives, their futures uncertain. Many of the single ladies were going to register at the labour exchange to make munitions.

---

[50] King Zog had a reputation for smoking up to 200 cigarettes per day.

[51] The Women's Voluntary Society provided personnel for essential civil defence work, rising to one million members during wartime. Officers served as ARP wardens; accompanied child evacuees; ran field kitchens and centres for those made homeless in the Blitz; helped salvage items from bombed premises; ran clothing banks for people who had lost everything; ran car pools and local travel services; offered refreshments to military personnel in transit; and provided domestic support such as cleaning, a cheery smile and a nice cup of tea in settings such as hospitals.

I was uncertain about what to do next. I had given it very little thought, but I did not want to be a burden on my children. At last I made up my mind. I would go to the insurance office to claim some compensation for my losses.

They would have none of it. Apparently there was an exclusion in my policy for 'Acts of War', and thus they were cleared of all responsibility. But at least I have my contract with the Reids and that will at least replace my car and some of my possessions.

By now it was noon. I desperately needed a new blouse. I have been wearing the same one for over a week and I dare not describe its condition. I bought a blouse which will serve me for now, but which I know will be useless to me afterwards. Now that I have found a room in a hotel, I intend to sleep for as long as possible, no longer disturbed by the snoring of a companion, and the pitch and yaw of the ship.

Saturday 28th June

I woke this morning, washed, had breakfast, and made my way to the railway station.

The train was packed with refugees and returning nationals like myself. I managed to secure a window seat and sat staring at the countryside rushing by. I had been longing to see the white cliffs, green fields, and orchards full of fruit. It was like passing through a desert, scorched yellow, with no fodder for the winter. The guard told me there had been a great heatwave to match my own in the South of France.

When we arrived at Paddington, I stood for a minute or two on the platform as the crowd pushed and jostled as they passed me by. I don't know how to explain what I sensed at that moment. I knew that I was home, but without Will here by my side, it felt like the end of the world.

A New Normal

1940–1959

Unwilling to impose herself on her children, Kate caught a train for Cambridge, hoping that she might be able to stay at Atholl Lodge, her last home, as a tenant of Dr Cott, who had bought it from Will and Kate. Their turntable summer house[52], which could be rotated to follow the sun and avoid the wind, and in which Kate had often slept in the summer, had not been part of the purchase and was awaiting removal when they returned to England. When she arrived, she found the house locked and empty.

She went to Hockeys, the agency that had handled the sale, who explained that Dr Cott was now working for the war effort, developing camouflage, and had rented the house to an Indian gentleman who had not yet moved in. Kate persuaded Hockeys to buy the summer house and then went off in search of accommodation.

All of the hotels and boarding houses were full. She ended up in a large cellar with a kitchen, whose owners had started taking in boarders. The other residents were evacuees from London and students attending the Cambridge Summer Schools. They had their own put-up beds and ate communally at a long table.

Determined to occupy herself, Kate enrolled at one of the Summer Schools at Girton College – a Women's European gathering that was already in session. She made friends with a Latvian schoolmistress and a lady from Helsingfors in Finland. She seemed content during

---

[52] Presumably based on George Bernard Shaw's revolving summerhouse which was widely copied during the early twentieth century.

this time, and the only reminder of war that she recorded was a bomb that fell on St Paul's Catholic Church in Cambridge.

When the course ended, Kate wrote to her son Bill, telling him and her daughter-in-law, Lorna, that she was coming to see them and hoped that he was not too busy to receive her. Bill was waiting for her on the platform at Durham Station, in darkness made even more sinister by the blackout regulations.

Bill and Lorna's welcome, and their reunion, must have been intense, their happiness tinged with sorrow at the loss of Will, but tempered by Kate's first sight of her grandson, also a Will. Kate went straight to bed and slept long into the following morning.

The following day, Lorna and Bill gave a dinner party in what Kate describes as '. . . the English Style, involving a large piece of roast'. All of her immediate family were there, including her daughter Barbara's fiancé, Pilot Officer John Day, a South African lecturer who had come to England to join RAF Bomber Command, and fight for Britain and the Empire.[53]

Bill told Kate that after leaving St Jean de Luz, he had been ten days travelling before he finally made it back to England, and that by an amazing coincidence, he had met the New Zealand couple, the Muirs, on the train from Paris, and the three of them had travelled together to England.

Kate enjoyed a long rest, three weeks of which she said she spent in bed. She then made a journey to her

---

[53] Three months after this meal took place, John Day took part in a daring raid over Norway and was awarded the DFC for his role in achieving a direct hit on the target under intense enemy fire. He was injured when his damaged plane crash-landed in the Hebrides. One of his legs was amputated. The newspapers of the day reported Barbara's desperate dash north to be at his side. John walked down the aisle on an artificial leg on 12th August 1942, when he and Barbara were married at Lamesley Parish Church, County Durham. John returned to flying duties, but sadly did not survive the war.

177

permanent home, Wigton Hall, in Cumbria, intending to move back in temporarily whilst preparing it for sale.

She was terribly upset on finding that the tenants had neglected the buildings and allowed the gardens to go wild. It had not helped that the head gardener left in charge was now working at Kirkbride at a factory assembling and repairing aeroplanes.[54]

The current tenants' lease on the Hall had expired, but they were refusing to leave until they found suitable accommodation in the location of their choice. Kate sought legal advice and was told it would be a long and difficult process to evict them. All accommodation in Wigton had been taken up by evacuees from Newcastle, foreign refugees, and engineers working for the government at the Kirkbride factory.

Ever resourceful, Kate returned to Bill and Lorna's home in Flawsworth to purchase a caravan she had noticed for sale in a nearby farmyard. The owner had joined the army and gone off to fight. Almost brand new, it was a caravan de luxe, designed for holidays and weekend fishing trips. It held seventy gallons of fresh water and was very roomy. Kate had it towed to Wigton Hall and parked it close to the old pigeon loft and a cart shed. She bought an old perambulator-type Austin 7 from Bill, and set off, determined to make herself a nuisance until the tenants finally gave up and moved out. Not long afterwards, one of the tenants died – not through Kate's fault, although she confessed that she felt bad '. . . because I had prayed for it!' The other tenants then left.

Kate was joined by her daughter Dorothy, and they lived together in the West Wing, while bringing the rest of the property to a habitable state, prior to putting it up for sale. While doing so, they drew on Kate's experience

---

[54] Kirkbride Airfield was opened in May 1939 as a storage and maintenance base for aircraft, from which they were delivered to active units by pilots of the Air Transport Auxiliary, set up at what is now the White Heather Hotel. The airfield was closed in 1960.

on her father's farm and kept poultry and cattle on the land.

During this period, Kate made a number of attempts to persuade Walter Reid to deliver on his promise to provide her with a car and additional compensation for the loss of her possessions, as agreed in the formal contract. He sent her a cheque for £15, which she did not cash, but did not respond to her request for a replacement car. When it was apparent that he had no intention of honouring that part of the contract, she took him to court. The whole of the case was well documented in all of the major newspapers at the time, under headlines that included:

REFUGEES 'LIKE A FLOOD'
FRENCH ADVENTURE
Daily Telegraph, 4th April 1941

CAR LOST IN FRANCE
OWNER SUES HONEYMOON COUPLE
ECHO OF JUNE DISASTER
Scotsman, 23rd March 1941

BRIDE 'GRATEFUL' TO WIDOW
ESCAPE FROM NAZIS
Daily Telegraph, 24th April 1941

HONEYMOON PAIR'S ESCAPE
AS HUNS INVADED FRANCE
WOMAN'S HIGH COURT CLAIM
Irish News, 25th March 1941

Walter Joseph Reid was at that time a second lieutenant in the Royal Artillery, and gave his address as the Royal Automobile Club. The case took a number of days and, following a long preamble outlining the way in which Kate and the Reids had come together, quickly homed in on the nature of the written agreements between them. Walter Reid maintained that there had been a second agreement written on a different piece of paper, in which he had offered to replace Kate's car with his own MG sports car (worth £250). That agreement appeared to have disappeared, although he claimed that Kate had referred to his MG sports car in her correspondence with him.

The case now turned on the one existing written agreement and, in particular, on the deletion of the following sentence:

> *'The car I shall replace by a new one of the latest model, and the same horse power and type.'*

And its replacement with the following:

> *'I shall pay a fair price for the things Mrs Powell was obliged to throw away to make room for us in the car, viz.: the sum of £15.'*

Walter Reid claimed that the changes had been made with Kate's knowledge and agreement, and that he had promised instead to give her his MG sports car. Kate claimed that she had never been made aware of the deletions, which must have been made while she was away from the car in Biarritz, when the Reids had the use of it to find them a hotel. The envelope had been in the glovebox with the other papers. She stated that she had posted it to Bill without having opened the envelope or re-read the agreement. She said she had been surprised on arriving at her son's house to discover that the agreement had been amended. Her barrister also pointed out that none of the amendments had been initialled by either Kate or Mr Powell.

Handwriting experts were called for the plaintiff and the defendant, both of whom arrived at opposite conclusions. Kate's expert stated that in his opinion the changes had been made with a different pen and a different ink from the original; Reid's expert disagreed.

Out of interest, I have included here a copy of the agreement as presented in court. The letters of the alphabet in the right-hand margin mark the sections analysed by the handwriting experts.

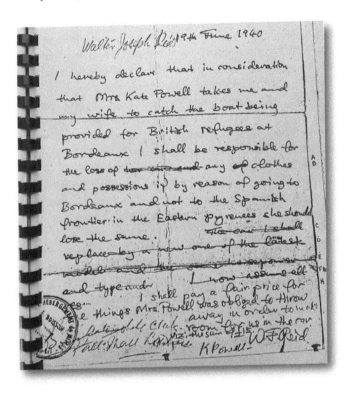

On 25th April 1941, in the High Court of Justice King's Bench Division at The Old Bailey, Mr Justice Cassels found in favour of Kate Powell. He was disinclined to accept that Mr Reid had dishonestly altered the agreement, and concluded that Mr Reid had acted honourably, and that there had been a misunderstanding that might be explained by Mrs Powell's recollection having been affected by '... the tragic and unhappy experience through which she had passed.'

In a judgement worthy of King Solomon, he said that he believed that the plaintiff and the defendant had both given honest testimony. His view was that Mrs Powell was clearly entitled to recover compensation from the defendant for her losses. Rather than the £575 she sought, he awarded her £400, to include her car and the £15 stated in the agreement as the cost of the belongings she had been forced to leave behind. He also awarded her the costs of bringing the case, less the costs resulting from the involvement of both handwriting experts.

In 1942, Kate sold Wigton Hall to the British Rayophane factory[55], to whom the other two wings had by then been let to house their managers. They moved to a flat in Chatsworth Square, Carlisle, until buying Fiddleback Farm[56], four miles from Carlisle, in 1947.

In the same year, before moving into Fiddleback Farm, Barbara and Kate returned to Provence to visit Will's grave. Barbara described their visit to her Aunt Marie, Kate's sister.

'After the war I took Mother back to find Father's grave. We stayed in a hotel in Nice that Mother had chosen, not for much money, it being out of season. It had beautiful rooms and was right on the Front. We went by train. We were taken to the graveyard by a very nice man. I think it must have been the Mr Birman mentioned in Mother's diary. His car was a wartime basic type, scarcely more than a box. Mr Birman had known Father, and also Bill, perhaps from when Bill and Lorna had been on their honeymoon, or more likely when Bill had come back to

---

[55] The factory originally produced artificial cellulose film, but changed its output to make rayon, or 'artificial silk'. Its modern successor, Innovia Films, is the largest employer in Wigton, remains based at and around the Hall, and still creates specialist cellophane and wraps for packaging and labelling.

[56] Fiddleback Farm lies on the site of a Roman mile station en route to Hadrian's Wall. In the early 18th century, an eccentric owner rebuilt the main house in the shape of a violin, and other structures as an accordion and a banjo, the latter sadly pulled down in the 1920s.

St Max to try to persuade Mother and Father to return, after the outbreak of war (at Dunkirk time).

The journey to the graveyard was a few miles from St Max, travelling upwards at an angle, I think to the left. Over the wall was a wonderful view of the Mediterranean. It was all very beautiful and wild still – like the Maquis – and the Genesta (wild broom) was everywhere. Now I imagine there has been much more building of villas.

We found the grave, and there was a gravestone for William Powell. A nice simple thing, and a glass cover for some artificial flowers on the grave.

Mr Birman remained further away. We stood for a while and Mother wiped one eye – her only demonstration.

I think Mother had been through too much to cry, but I left her there and went to see the verger in his little place, there being no church there that I recall. I discovered that it was our friend Sydney Aston who had been here and put up the gravestone. He must have come almost straight after the war.'

Fiddleback had been let to a market gardener who had become too old to manage it effectively. Both the business and the farm were run down and sadly neglected. Barbara, now widowed, left the Women's Auxiliary Air Force, and went to live with her mother and sister.

The three of them, with the assistance of German prisoners of war, set about completely restoring Fiddleback Farm, its buildings, and the business. At the end of the war, Kate's other daughter, Nancy, returned from Germany where she had been working in Army Intelligence. With the sum of £2,000 given to each of the three daughters by their brother Bill – from the inheritance he had received from Will – Nancy set up a poultry business with thousands of pedigree chicks, and Barbara bought cattle, pigs and geese, and ran the market garden, utilising a number of large greenhouses. Nancy's business failed due to the lack of mains electricity, which meant that her large incubators proved too costly to run. She went to keep house for the granddaughters of the Earl of Carlisle, with whom she became very friendly. One of them – Winifred – married the artist Ben Nicholson, and was a fine artist in her own right, having an exhibition of her work at the Tate Gallery.

Fiddleback Farm, circa early 1954
Kate (seated), Paddy the gardener, a 'bob-a-job' Scout,
and Kate's daughter Barbara

The country idyll at Fiddleback Farm was shattered for Kate by the news of the death of her son Bill in 1951 at the age of 45, and then again in 1954 by that of her daughter Dorothy, at the age of 52. Barbara reported that Kate was in such a depressed state following Dorothy's death that she could not even bring herself to change her underclothes.

Kate was never quite the same after this and spent a lot of time in bed downstairs, while Barbara worked all day on the farm.

In 1959, Kate became anxious that Barbara would be left with all of the cost of the maintenance of Fiddleback, on which – as was the practice with all of Will and Kate's previous properties – there was a mortgage, and so decided that they should move to somewhere smaller. A more or less derelict property – Rowan Lea on Church Lane in Thursby – came up for auction. Kate took a taxi with a friend, Mrs Banks, to the auction and bought the property in Barbara's name. Barbara took out a mortgage that covered the property in its present state, and secured a teaching post at the high school, leaving Mrs Banks and her sister Nancy, who came back to live with her, to set about gutting it and installing electricity. Barbara and Tommy Martin, the gardener from Fiddleback, cut down the orchard and began work on the garden.

That winter, before completion of the work, Kate passed away at Fiddleback Farm, aged eighty-one.

In 1962, Barbara went on a prolonged camping holiday, ending up in Sainte Maxime. She visited her father's grave for the final time, taking her mother's ashes with her. She arranged for the stonemason to add her mother's name, as well as that of Dorothy, to the headstone.

Kate at last was reunited with her beloved Will and their story was complete.

Author's Note

Will's diary was a journal written for his family, to tell them about his journey to New Zealand in 1893, and to reassure them that he had arrived safely. Consequently, it is a vivid and detailed contemporary account of his adventure that required very little intervention on my part. My only role has been to annotate some of the references within the journal for a 21st-century readership.

Kate's diary was written in France forty-seven years later, while in her sixty-second year. She recorded events in faint pencil as they unfolded, and later by recollection. Fifty years later, it was typed up by Barbara, one of her daughters. Kate's diary, just fifty-six pages in length, appears to have been written both for herself and for her children. Mundane at first, the entries became increasingly desperate as the Germans advanced and escape routes began to close. So familiar was she with her surroundings that she felt little need to describe them, and I gained the impression that it was not in her nature to dwell, or to elaborate on her emotions, although there were tantalising glimpses of these when she was at her most wretched.

According to Barbara, the only occasion on which Kate was observed to have shown any outward sign of grief at the loss of Will was when Barbara took her back to France to visit his grave in 1947. Even then it amounted to no more than the wiping of a single tear from her eye. However, when Kate's daughter Dorothy died at the age of fifty-two, hard on the heels of her brother Bill, we do know that she was wracked by grief and became severely depressed. We are also told that Kate wept when Will refused to allow their daughter Lorna to go up to Girton College, Oxford, on the grounds that they could not afford the fees.

As well as hints to her emotional state, Kate provided clues in her diary to the idyllic life that she and her beloved husband led in the South of France in the months and days immediately before the outbreak of the Second World War, and a slightly more detailed account of her struggle to escape the advancing Axis Forces. Some of the original diary was illegible, and several parts had clearly been written out of sequence. This required some research on my part to piece together the scattered elements and provide a little of the historical context.

In an attempt to bring Kate's story alive, I tried to fill in some of those missing elements and to do justice to her complex personality. In many ways, the process resembled how I imagine it must feel to attempt to invisibly mend a precious tapestry.

I included all of Kate's snippets of dialogue, with modest stylistic adjustments, and amended a couple of comments typical of a person of her time, but not acceptable in our own.

I followed all of the events as they occurred and tried to stay true to Kate's telling of her story. I believe that it represents a fascinating personal account of a seminal moment in history. I hope that you enjoyed Kate's story as much as I did in bringing it to life.

The accounts of Will's life following his return from New Zealand, Kate's early life before their first meeting, their years together, and Kate's experiences following her return from France up to the time of her death, are based on comprehensive notes written by her daughter, Barbara Day, together with brief notes written by Kate's sister Ruth, and my own research.

Acknowledgements

Margaret Jack and Julia Guttridge (the family archivist), who jointly inherited the Powell Diaries, for permission to publish Will's journal, to work on their Great-Aunt Kate's diary, and to reproduce the photographs of Will and Kate, along with additional material collated by Will and Kate's daughter Barbara, and Kate's sister Ruth. Alex Jack who brought the diaries to me in the hope that I might make them more widely accessible. Geoff Smith at the Lutterworth Museum for permission to reproduce photographs of the barque SS *Lutterworth*. Dr John R A Cleaver, Life Fellow and College Archivist, Fitzwilliam College, Cambridge, for information relating to 74 Storey's Way. John Percival, for genealogical information on Kate Percival's wider family history. My Editor, Monica Byles, for her wise and incisive suggestions, her eagle eye, and her consummate copy-editing skills.

And, above all, Will and Kate Powell to whom this book really belongs.

Bill Rogers. June 2021

ALSO BY BILL ROGERS

DCI TOM CATON
MANCHESTER MURDER MYSTERIES

The Cleansing
The Head Case
The Tiger's Cave
A Fatal Intervention
Bluebell Hollow
A Trace of Blood
The Frozen Contract
Backwash
A Venetian Moon
Angel Meadow
The Girl and the Shadowman
The Opportunist

JOANNE STUART
NATIONAL CRIME AGENCY SERIES

The Pick, The Spade And The Crow
The Falcon Tattoo
The Tangled Lock
The Blow Out

INDIVIDUAL WORKS
Teenage and Young Adult Fiction
The Cave
Short Crime Stories
Breakfast at Katsouris
Eight walks based on the Manchester crime novels
Caton's Manchester

About the Author

Photo: Paul Whur, 2015

Bill Rogers has written sixteen crime novels to date, all of them based in and around the City of Manchester. Twelve feature DCI Tom Caton and his team, set in and around Manchester, while four novels in a spin-off series feature SI Joanne Stuart on secondment to the Behavioural Sciences Unit at the National Crime Agency, located in Salford Quays.

Formerly a teacher, education inspector, and Head of the Manchester Schools Improvement Service, Bill worked for the National College for School Leadership before retiring to begin his writing career. Born in London, Bill has four generations of Metropolitan Police behind him. He is married with two adult children and lives close to the City of Manchester.

For more information, and to contact Bill, send him an email, or visit his Amazon author page:

billrogers@billrogers.co.uk
amazon.co.uk/-/e/B0034NWVC0